A PRACTICAL GUIDE

VOIP

FOR THE NON-TELEPHONE ENGINEER

Joe Yeung
5/1/2015

References:-
TeleGeography - (published by WSJ.D *15 January 2015*)
Wikipedia - (wikipedia.org)
Easy Office Phone - (easyofficephone.com)
InteropNet Labs

ISBN 978-1-326-26063-7

CONTENTS

ABOUT THIS BOOK

This book is not about Voice Over Internet Protocol technology, nor is it about the history of VOIP. It is designed to be a practical guide to the implementation of a telephone system that is based on the VOIP technology. If you like, it is like a workshop guide to installing a VOIP system for a small business enterprise. The guide is written for the reasonably IT (information technology) literate and not for the specialists. In other words, I hope to take you, as a non telephony specialist, through the processes of implementing a VOIP system that will allow your organisation to benefit from a VOIP system.

WHO SHOULD READ THIS BOOK?

If you are an owner or manager of a small organisation that is looking to change your telephone system, or maybe you are only interested in whether VOIP is appropriate for your organisation, you will benefit from reading this book. Remember, VOIP is not necessarily a must have for any organisation, it is just a very cost effective and feature rich communication system that most organisations will benefit from having!

I DON'T KNOW ANYTHING ABOUT VOIP

For those who need a little bit of history of VOIP and how it works, please refer to the chapter 9 to get a brief background of the technology to help you understand VOIP. Please try to not get too bogged down with the technology, your interest should be focused on the benefits and pitfalls of VOIP for your organisation. In particular, you need to be able to compare the benefits against its pitfalls and make an informative decision about the business case for VOIP.

I DON'T KNOW ANYTHING ABOUT SIP (SESSION INITIATED PROTOCOL)

Once again, reading chapter 9 will give you a basic understanding of the SIP protocol. Hopefully, you will no longer be confused by SKYPE™ and SIP.

I DON'T KNOW ANYTHING ABOUT TCP/IP (TRANSMISSION CONTROLLED PROTOCOL/ INTERNET PROTOCOL)

This guide includes all the basic TCP/IP settings you will need to install and configure a VOIP system. Although this guide does not pretend to teach you TCP/IP, you will still benefit from it with the basic understanding of TCP/IP and VOIP.

I AM NOT PARTICULARLY TECHNICAL

You are in luck, whilst you need some degree of technical competence in IT, the guide is written to be like the assembly instructions of a flat packed bookcase, you need to follow instructions and have the skills to put it together, but you do not need to know why it should be assembled in a certain way. If you are not comfortable doing it yourself, employ a specialist firm to do it for you. At least by the time you have finished reading this, you will have a good understanding of why, how and what a VOIP system is all about.

DO I HAVE TO USE THE SAME EQUIPMENT AND SERVICES IN THE GUIDE?

Absolutely not! Although specific equipment and services may have been used as examples (this guide is based on a real and successful installation) , you can choose your own system as long as your equipment is designed to achieve the same tasks. You can do this because most of the components can be configured in a similar way via web interfaces, so as long as you know a bit about TCP/IP, you should be able to configure those equipment correctly. Having said the above, it pays to consider using services and equipment proven to work together rather than trial and error.

WHAT IF I DON'T USE THE SAME SERVICES OR EQUIPMENT IN THIS GUIDE?

If you want to use your own service providers and different equipment, please make sure your suppliers are specialists in this field. Try not to consider products and services purely on price alone, it is more important to purchase an appropriate product or service that is well supported and reliable in operation.

CHAPTER 1

THE SCENARIO

For this guide to reflect a more realistic business situation, I have created a fictitious company whose business is to sell professional services to organisations throughout the UK. The main aim of this scenario is to allow you (the reader) to draw parallels with your requirements to that of my company. The assumption is that you are reading this guide because your organisation is either looking to replace your current telephone system or you are looking to install a new telephone system.

Although the company is fictitious, the telephone system implementation is based mostly on a successful installation of a VOIP system. Some extra functions are added to the system for illustration purposes and to add to the benefits you may be looking for, but the basic system is a successful working system that is fulfilling the business needs of its owners.

THE COMPANY

Let's call our company ACME Ltd., the company was set up 5 years ago by its current owner Mr. John Smith. The company has been successfully providing a business reporting service for small to medium size businesses. The business has been expanding gradually over the past years with the help of John's wife Mary, who is very focused on the management of the business. In addition, she is very competent in IT and is responsible for the smooth operation of their company network. Mary is the sort of person who is willing to ask questions and research into business and IT issues in order to help the business.

Due to business expansion, the company has negotiated new premises in the city centre of Newcastle upon Tyne and Mary is asked to manage the implementation of a telephone system that is appropriate for the expanding business and at a cost that the company can afford.

Before Mary makes any decisions on what telephone systems to consider, she has decided to review the company's current situation with regards to telephony needs first.

COMPANY STAFF

The company currently employs twenty staff, twelve of which are based locally and will be operating in the new premises. They have a small branch office based in Amersham to service clients in and around London and the south east. Five staff members are permanently based in the branch office whilst three are remote workers who work from home. They currently use both their mobile and their home telephones for business calls.

Due to the success of employing remote home based staff, the company is planning to expand their operations by increasing the number of home based staff to cover a wider area.

The company pays a portion of their monthly bills. Since it is too time consuming to separate out private and business calls, the figures are not accurate and do not necessarily reflect the actual costs incurred. The current system works as follows:-

HOME WORKERS

- individual staff have their home and mobile number printed on their business cards
- clients communicate with individual staff either using their home number or their mobile
- if client cannot communicate directly with staff, they leave messages on their answer phone
- individual staff reports to main office on the main office number
- main office communicates with staff on their mobile or home number

Although this system has worked up until now, there are some issues that are very obvious and should really be addressed fully. The issues are as follows:-

- if a member of staff leaves, some clients may have problems contacting the company as the staff is the main point of contact
- if a member of staff leaves for a competitor, the company may lose a lot of business

- calls to remote staff received by main office cannot be transferred to staff directly
- as the staff are out most of the time, contacting them tends to be difficult
- most staff are not too happy to give out their home number
- business calls to staff homes tend not to be well received by their family
- making or receiving business calls at home interferes with family's usage
- remote staff has to go through main switchboard to call internal staff
- company has no knowledge or control over staff calls or voice messages
- the company's contribution to the remote staff's telephone usage is subjected to questions regularly

There has been discussions on installing a landline for every remote worker and paying for unlimited calls for both their landlines as well as their mobiles, however, there are still the issues of making calls to mobiles from their landlines and making calls to national numbers like 0845 and 0870 etc. that needs to be addressed. In addition, there are still issues like:-

- must remote staff use mobile for mobile calls and landline for landline calls?
- what if the remote staff is out and has to call national numbers which are payable because they are outside the mobile tariff
- who is responsible for the landline and unlimited call packages when a remote staff leaves

The above issues are mainly financial and do not address any of the issues involving operational difficulties like transferring calls to remote workers and calls disturbing the family etc.

The most important issue that concerns John and Mary is that of a remote staff leaving for a competitor, as this will almost certainly have an impact on their business and they have absolutely no control over the issue at all. They need more control over their communication system and they need to manage the communication flow much better if they want to address this issue effectively.

MAIN OFFICE STAFF

Besides John and Mary, there will be ten other staff operating from the new main office in town. Their job titles and functions are as follow:-

- John is the MD and is responsible for all aspects of running the business
- Mary is the office manager responsible for the operations side of the business
- the accountant - she is responsible for all aspects of the business finances as well as payroll
- telephone researchers - there are two researchers responsible for calling businesses on behalf of the company's clients
- report writers - there are two specialists who are responsible for creating business surveys and providing analysis
- sales - there are two sales persons who use the main office as base but are out most of the time
- secretaries - there are two secretaries responsible for creating and typing reports for all clients
- telephone system operator and receptionist - responsible for answering all calls and handling all visitors to the main office

THE CURRENT SYSTEM

Main Office

There are currently twelve staff operating at their current location. The telephone system is a conventional PBX (Private Branch Exchange) with four ISDN (Integrated Service Digital Network) lines and twelve extensions. The telephone system operates reliably and provides very good quality telephone calls.

Remote Office

There are currently five staff operating at their Amersham office. Like the main office, the system is a conventional PBX with two ISDN lines.

The company currently pays a monthly rental plus quarterly maintenance to the telephone company that supplied the system. All calls are routed through this supplier at a rate that is lower than the standard rate of BT (British Telecom).

The current telephone system for the main office was installed when the company was formed and has worked quite reliably since. The telephone system for the branch office was installed three years ago, by the same telephone supplier using the same service provider for all calls.

At the time, it seemed the right thing to do. The current telephone system supplier provided the best quote with regards to initial cost, call and maintenance costs and services offered.

As the current telephone system provider was the original provider for the company's telephone system, it seemed logical for Mary to have chosen them for their branch office when the branch office was opened. The cost quoted then was not even challenged as no other suppliers was asked to quote anyway.

However, there are some issues that are making Mary unhappy with it now, they are:-

- four lines is no longer enough for the main office - for the current level of usage (two of the lines are almost permanently in use by the telephone researchers), scheduled and future expansion will mean serious issues with both incoming and outgoing calls
- same goes for the branch office with only two lines
- some telephone companies are offering better call rates, in particular, mobile calls, but this system is restricted to using the current telephone service provider, hence the telephone bills are much higher than necessary
- no music on hold - beeping noises instead of music on hold reflects badly on the professional image of the company
- no voicemail - the lack of voicemail means the receptionist has to note down messages and later email them to the staff, taking

up valuable time and sometimes forgetting to send the message all together

- no integration between offices - all inter office calls are made as if they are external calls
- no integration with remote staff - when remote workers call, they need to go through reception, tying up reception and using up one of the lines.
- calls between offices cannot be transferred
- calls between offices has to go through reception, thus wasting reception time
- external calls for remote users cannot be transferred directly to them
- no telephone logs - for management purposes, it is a negative point
- call to remote users costs the company the same as external standard calls

SIMPLE DIAGRAM SHOWING OPERATION OF THE CURRENT TELEPHONE SYSTEM

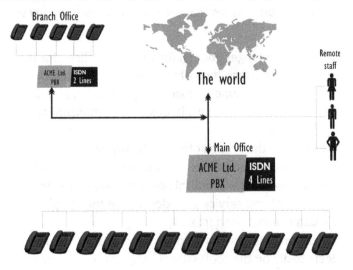

Looking at the telephone bills, Mary has come up with a startling conclusion, they are paying a lot more for their usage in comparison to what is available on the market. Although the price of calls charged by their supplier is at a lower rate than the standard BT charges, they do not take into account any deals offered by BT. On contacting different call providers, she discovered that massive savings can be achieved by changing their current telephone system and provider.

In order to help her understand the situation better, she built herself a small spreadsheet based on her current bill to analyse their telephone costs.

The table is based on the monthly expenditure from the telephone service provider. The cost of telephone system maintenance and the rental system itself is not included.

MONTHLY TELEPHONE EXPENDITURE TABLE:

Head office

	Units	Duration (mins)	Avg. call duration (mins)	Total call costs in p	Avg call costs in p	Unit cost	Total £
No. of ISDN lines	4					12.50	50.00
Broadband	1					10.67	10.67
Fax Lines	1					12.33	12.33
Outing calls	8756	18777.00	2.14	46406.80	5.30		464.07
Fax outgoing	161			1707.00		10.60	17.07
Ip address							2.00
						Total	556.14

Branch Office

	Units	Duration (mins)	Avg. call duration (mins)	Total call costs in p	Avg call costs in p	Unit cost	Total £
No. of ISDN lines	2					12.50	25.00
Broadband	1					10.67	10.67
Fax Lines	1					12.33	12.33
Outing calls	4280	9553.00	2.23	35096.00	8.20		350.96
Fax outgoing	23			183.00		7.96	1.83
						Total	400.79

Remote workers

	No. of staff					Contribution £	Total £
Remote staff	3					20.00	60.00

Total current monthly expenditure on telephone and internet usage	£1,016.93

Although Mary did not have a complete breakdown of every call, she has estimated that over £400 per month is spent of calling mobile numbers from the two offices. When the service provider quoted a call rate of 7p per minute, it sounded very reasonable when compared to standard BT rates. However, when she compared that to mobile call plans, it becomes very expensive.

Clearly, she can call client mobiles from her own mobile phone that would make calls significantly cheaper, as her tariff is a fixed monthly payment of £15 with unlimited number of calls to mobiles and standard landline numbers.

Now I am not suggesting for one moment that one mobile is all you need to cover the thousands of minutes of calls made by all staff, but it illustrates the fact that using a SIM (subscriber identity module) package to make mobile calls are much cheaper. On any account, for a professional business, it is not viable to use one mobile hand set and make all staff use it for mobile calls. As their telephone system routes all calls through their current provider, they have no other choice but to make all calls via their service provider.

Like most small business owners and managers, when the requirement of a telephone system was considered, Mary just asked several local companies to supply quotes and she did the negotiations and made her choice based on her own business and communication skills. There is no doubt that she had made a very good business decision in acquiring a telephone system that she had chosen and at the very competitive price.

When the branch office opened, she chose a supplier (the same supplier that supplied the first system) that she was able to work with, at a cost that she considered reasonable, so it was a sound business decision too.

CHAPTER 2

VOICE OVER INTERNET PROTOCOL (VOIP) - THE MISCONCEPTIONS

VOIP must be the most misunderstood term in business telecommunication. When we mention VOIP, most people will think it is about using the internet to make free telephone calls. Some common misconceptions of VOIP besides making free internet calls are:-

- it is about SKYPE™
- call quality is poor
- you need the internet to make calls
- it is for home use only
- VOIP telephones must be plugged into the back of a PC
- you can only call people using the same type of system
- you need an adaptor for every telephone to link to the internet
- you need specialists to install VOIP telephone systems
- you cannot use broadband for VOIP
- VOIP is unreliable
- VOIP is for large organisations only

To be brutally honest, there is an element of truth in all the above. If a comment is commonly made, then there must be some truth in it. On the other hand, if it is a misconception, then why do people think otherwise?

VOIP IS ABOUT USING SKYPE™

According to telecommunications research company TeleGeography (published by WSJ.D *15 January 2015*) " SKYPE™'s traffic was almost 40% the size of the entire conventional international telecom market". With market size such as this, no wonder most people think of VOIP as SKYPE™.

Although SKYPE™ has a large share of the VOIP market, it does not mean VOIP is SKYPE™! It is the same as saying the world wide web is a major part of the internet, but the internet does not mean only the world wide web. SKYPE™ uses its own proprietary protocol instead of the industry standard SIP protocol, as a result, you cannot call a SKYPE™

user without using SKYPE™ or using special software like SKYPE™ for your computer or functions from your standard VOIP system e.g. [1]SISkyEE or [2]SKYPE Connect. Conversely, for a SKYPE user to call normal telephone numbers, you need to use [3]SKYPE out and you have to pay for these calls.

For a business, it is sometimes desirable to be able to call SKYPE™ users from your telephone system and allow SKYPE™ users to call you for free from their system. However, you will need a telephone system that supports SKYPE™ Connect (unless you have SKYPE™ installed on all the users computers), this will incur a cost for your business as there is a channel subscription charge for each SIP Profile, based on the number of concurrent call channels that you buy for that SIP Profile. Of course, if you call standard telephone or mobile numbers using SKYPE out, there will be the usual per minute call charges too.

The advantages of using SKYPE™ are:-

- SKYPE™ to SKYPE™ calls are free
- SKYPE out call charges are low in comparison to our main telephone services providers like BT or Virgin, especially international calls
- SKYPE™ is used by a large number of people and hence by using SKYPE™, you can easily reach a large audience
- for a business, SKYPE™ buttons on a website makes it very convenient for SKYPE™ users to contact you

---

Note

[1]SISKyEE is a business solution that allows you to link your SIP PBX to SKYPE™ users

[2] SKYPE™Connect allows your existing SIP-enabled PBX to connect to SKYPE™ users.

[3] SKYPE Out allows SKYPE™ users to call standard phone lines

---

On the other hand, there are some disadvantages of using SKYPE™ too, they are:-

- requirement to use SKYPE™ service and compatible equipment, hence extra cost
- closed system and cannot be reached by standard equipment unless add-ons are used
- requirement for a reliable and good quality internet connection

For any business that wants to attract clients with SKYPE™ systems especially those from overseas, having SKYPE™ or a system connected to SKYPE™ makes it much easier for clients to contact them.

From a marketing point of view, allowing SKYPE™ users to easily contact your business also makes sense. However, if your business does not intend to attract SKYPE™ users or use SKYPE™ connection as a marketing point, there is little merit in using SKYPE™ as you are likely to get much better return on investment by using an industry standard SIP based system.

CALL QUALITY IS POOR

In order to challenge this misconception, we need to understand what governs the quality of VOIP calls. Your voice quality will be poor if you are using the following:-

- poor quality handset - especially if you are using a USB (Universal Serial Bus) handset that is plugged into the USB port of computer
- poor internet connection - if you only use the internet to make calls and you have a very poor internet connection
- poor service provider - the quality of voice calls are heavily dependent on the service provider you use, remember, not all providers are created equal
- poor quality equipment - besides handsets or desk phones, your PBX and any gateways that connects you to standard telephone lines and mobile services matter a great deal to the call quality

- incorrectly configured equipment - VOIP equipment tends to be extremely configurable, it is very easy to configure them incorrectly
- local network conditions - like all data, VOIP data is carried by the local area network which also carries business data. Under some circumstances, the network may suffer adverse conditions which will affect the quality of VOIP calls
- users misconception - it is common for some people to think that just because a few calls have been affected by circumstances which affected the call quality adversely, VOIP call quality is bad

Although I called the above a misconception, it is real if your circumstances happen to be one or more of those mentioned above. If you use a service provider that offers low quality calls, it is extremely likely that you will often get poor quality calls. It is no comfort to you if you have quality issues with your VOIP system, misconception or not.

Most of us nowadays have mobile phones, we all have suffered quality issues from time to time, but we still use them. Why do we still use mobile phones? We use mobile phone because they are extremely handy, they allow us to make and receive calls from anywhere - as long as there is adequate coverage.

When the conditions are ideal, mobile calls are very good, good enough to clearly carry on a conversation without any danger of mishearing the other person. The problem is that conditions are not dictated by the mobile phone user. As an example, if a mobile caller is in a cafe where the person at the next table is talking very loudly, he may really struggle to hear the other person on his mobile, but that does not make mobile phone calls bad quality.

The issue about VOIP quality is not with the VOIP technology itself, it is all the factors that influence the call quality that the user experiences. As long as a VOIP system is designed to minimise external factors that cannot be controlled, it should be a system that supplies good quality calls consistently. If we use the mobile phone analogy as our guide, can we find any reason to not use VOIP if the benefits outweighs its shortcomings?

YOU NEED AN INTERNET CONNECTION TO USE VOIP

This is probably the most common misconception about VOIP at the moment. If you use any search engine to look up what VOIP means, chances are that you will find an answer like "VOIP is using the internet for making telephone calls".

The answer above is absolutely true, however, it is not the whole truth and can be misleading. You can certainly use VOIP over the internet to make telephone calls as many people do, but that is best described as Internet Telephony. The process of making telephone calls over the internet is exactly that, the fact the VOIP technology is used is only one aspect of it.

Having stated that we do not need internet to use VOIP, we must remind ourselves that we do need a functioning LAN (local area network) running TCP/IP. For most home users and a lot of small businesses, their internet router is what they use to connect their computers and VOIP equipment to the LAN. So if the router fails, their internet will also fail and so would their LAN. The result is that their VOIP system will not function as there is no functioning LAN.

In addition, VOIP (SIP) phones are produced with the assumption that they are connected to the internet and some will have the following functions:-

- Date time display
- Weather report
- Stock Market report

These functions require constant internet access to operate correctly. Although these functions are not crucial, without them, your telephone system will not really be working properly. Can you imagine how annoying it will be if your telephone is displaying the wrong date and time on the LCD screen all the time?

A lot of VOIP equipment will come with either ports to link them to standard telephone or ISDN lines, some will even have the ability to use mobile SIM cards to enable your VOIP system to make calls without going through the internet at all. Even low cost equipment may sometimes have one port called a lifeline which utilises a standard telephone line if the internet service fails.

Many people will ask "If VOIP does not require the internet, what is the point of using an internet protocol without using the internet then?" The short answer is - functionality and cost. We will cover this subject in detail later as this is the whole essence of this guide.

IT IS FOR HOME USE ONLY

Many home users have been benefitting from VOIP for quite some time now, the favourite use is for making free or low cost international calls to relatives overseas. With the explosive growth of the likes of SKYPE™ and Vonage etc., it is hardly surprising that people think of VOIP as a home users technology.

These service providers make it very simple for end users to set up and use their services either by installing software or plugging in an (ATA) analogue telephone adaptor to link a standard analogue telephone to the router.

If you consider how variable internet services are throughout the country and how variable the end users equipment can be, it is hardly surprising that call quality can also be variable too. They will range from crystal clear to almost unusable, but as home users trying to SKYPE™ relatives overseas for free, it is not a serious issue for them. Unfortunately for those who suffered bad quality calls, it will leave a bad taste and the idea that VOIP is low quality and only suitable for home users to get free or cheap calls.

For business users using typical telephone systems e.g. like having a PBX, their environment can be completely different, they have control over their own equipment and to a great extent, their service providers too.

VOIP TELEPHONES MUST BE PLUGGED INTO THE BACK OF A PC

It is very common for home users to attach a USB VOIP phone to the USB port of their computer to make calls over the internet e.g. SKYPE™. However, in general, their call quality tends to be very poor as these devices tend to be low cost and low quality. Better quality can quite often be achieved by using decent quality headsets and good sound boards on their systems. Unfortunately for a business environment, it is usually not practicable for constant use.

Industry standard (VOIP) SIP phones work perfectly without a computer, all they need is to be able to link to a PBX or SIP server either locally via LAN or over the internet. Some SIP phones have 2 network sockets which allow them to operate as a switch to link to the LAN as well as a computer simultaneously.

YOU NEED AN ADAPTOR TO LINK EVERY TELEPHONE TO THE INTERNET

By using what is commonly called an ATA (analogue to telephone adaptor), a user can connect a normal analogue telephone to an internet VOIP provider like Vonage etc. This process is fairly simple and the user can make calls to any valid telephone number as long as they have a package that covers the cost of calls.

Does that not mean you need an adaptor for every telephone you have? Obviously not! For any business, it is not sensible to have one telephone and one line for every single user. Unless you use a hosted solution (a SIP server/PBX on the internet), transferring of calls etc. which a business commonly requires will be very difficult.

In addition, the quality of calls may be affected by the quality of the ATA and how they are configured. Voice delays and echoes are quite common if the ATAs are not configured or working correctly.

For a business, it is more likely that either a hosted solution or a local PBX with standard SIP phones will be the norm. In this way, the business can control many aspects of their system and operation that is not available to the home user i.e. telephone quality and routing of calls etc.

You can only call people on the same service provider

Once again, this is not true. With the popularity of providers like SKYPE™ which allows users to make free calls to other SKYPE™ users, it is easy to see why people think they need the same service providers to make calls.

Unless a user wants to be tied to using a certain service provider only, it is sensible to subscribe to industry standard services providers (you can use more than one provider if your system allows you to do so). For any business, no matter how small it is, it is absolutely necessary to have more than one provider for back up or least cost routing (Least cost routing is the ability to make telephone calls using the cheapest provider by routing calls through that provider).

You need specialists to install a VOIP system

It is sensible to always use professionals to do a job. On the other hand, if you are comfortable with what you will be doing, then why not do it yourself?

This guide is written specifically to assist any IT literate person to make an informed decision on utilising VOIP and to actually plan and install a VOIP system without having to employ specialists. A user who has installed a SIP phone for home use has already got the initial understanding of VOIP and will be aware of how VOIP works. Planning and installing a VOIP system will just be the next logical step as the user will already know some of the steps involved.

Please remember, this guide is not written for people who want to implement a VOIP solution for a large organisation with hundreds of users, it is designed to help owners and managers of small businesses with only a handful of staff to do so if they wish.

You cannot use broadband for VOIP

VOIP will happily work with "broadband". The problem is that the quality of service of some internet providers' broadband service is variable. Unlike the plain old telephone service (POTS) where the call quality is fairly standard, VOIP is subjected to a lot of other variables which will affect its quality.

Contention ratio - Unless you subscribe to a special non-contented internet service, you will be sharing your internet connection with up to dozens of other users. If you happen to share your internet connection with users who upload and download a lot, your service will be seriously affected. This means that good VOIP quality will be extremely unlikely.

Upstream speed - Internet service providers love to quote very high downstream speed e.g. (often up to 16 Megabit). This is very misleading as it only tells us half the story. Whilst most internet service providers use (ADSL) asymmetric digital subscriber line technology to enable us to access the internet - the high quoted speed is only one way (downstream). Upstream speed (sending) is always a lot less, usually less than 1 Megabit.

Bearing in mind that a conversation is between 2 people, adequate speed for one way is no good. There is no point being able to hear perfectly clearly (downstream speed) for you if the person you are calling cannot hear you (upstream speed)! When you are having a conversation over the internet using VOIP, your downstream speed is limited by the upstream speed of your caller or the person you are calling. It is true for the person on the other side too, as his downstream is limited by your upstream speed. You can conclude that the important speed requirement is actually the upstream speed of your connection. So the normal high speed quoted by service providers becomes irrelevant as the upstream is more likely to influence the quality of your conversation.

In addition, there are other issues which will affect the speed of your internet connection that influences VOIP call quality e.g. your service provider or your equipment etc. The choice of service providers (internet and VOIP), the equipment and the network infrastructure are crucial to how well your VOIP system works).

VOIP IS UNRELIABLE
VOIP technology has been established for a long time now and the technology is well proven and reliable. What gives the perception that it is unreliable is what the VOIP system relies on to operate.

If you can afford it, a lease line with guaranteed speed (up and downstream) and a service level agreement will give you extremely reliable and good quality VOIP calls consistently. If the equipment and network infrastructure of your network is good, you can expect quality and reliability rivalling that of ISDN equivalent systems. Unfortunately, in the real world, your organisation needs serious investments and very high utilisation requirements to justify the investment and ongoing costs. For the purpose of this guide, we will disregard the above scenario as it is unlikely to be relevant to you.

Let us consider the factors which will affect the reliability of a VOIP system. Telephones - unlike a standard business telephone that is not capable of doing much, a VOIP /SIP Phone is actually run by a little microcomputer e.g. a Grandstream GXV3275 uses an ARMv7 (Advanced RISC Machines) processor with 825MB of RAM !! As such, just like your personal computer, it is possible for the system to fail if the software (firmware) is not well written. Although, it is often a simple task of restarting the telephone to get the system to work again. So the quality of the hardware, the software and how well it is configured governs how reliable your telephone operates.

Cabling - Very often, the VOIP phone will have dual network sockets allowing it to act as a switch to link one network socket to both telephone and personal computer. This increases the possibility for one of the cables to come loose (if the phone is moved) since most network (CAT5) cables are quite thick and inflexible.

If we compare the cables typically used for standard telephones and CAT5 network cables, it is obvious that the standard telephone cables are much thinner and more flexible, hence much easier to manage and tidy up. If you compare a VOIP phone that is also linked to a personal computer, with 2 thick network cables plus a power cable, it is much more difficult to manage and keep these cabling tidy and out of the way. The result is that these cables may come loose if the VOIP phone is moved about frequently, increasing the likelihood of the phone malfunctioning.

Routers and switches - If you are familiar with routers and switches, you will know that some of these devices frequently requires restarts (especially after a power cut). If your router that links you to the internet requires frequent restarts, it is not suitable for VOIP as it will cause the system to become unreliable.

For a lot of small networks, their internet router often act as the DHCP server (Dynamic Host Configuration Protocol) as well. This means that all the devices on the network acquire some of their configurations from the router, unreliability of the router will cause the VOIP system to become unreliable too. A typical scenario will be after a power cut, when power is restored, the VOIP system remains inoperable. This happens if the DHCP server on the router fails to restart, all the VOIP phones will not be able to acquire the network settings from the DHCP server on the router. As a result, the VOIP phones will effectively be not on the network and will therefore not work.

Once again, the failure of a router on a network has nothing to do with the reliability of VOIP. Unfortunately, as VOIP depends on a fully working and reliable network, this issue must be considered as part of any decision process.

VOIP providers - If internet telephony is a being used, then the reliability of the service provider must be crucial as some or all calls may be routed through them. Although most service providers claim to have almost 100% up time, it is prudent to think of some as better than others.

Internet service providers - Once again, if internet telephony is being used, the internet service provider is crucial too. Since some or all of the calls will be carried over the internet, the reliability of the internet service has to be the highest priority for the decision process.

Compatibility of equipment - Unlike a standard telephone system with proprietary hardware and software, VOIP utilises industry standard SIP compliant equipment. This means that VOIP is extremely flexible, but at the same time, it also allows for devices, software and equipment combinations that are not specifically designed to work together to be operating within the same system. This can sometimes lead to performance or reliability issues.

VOIP IS FOR LARGE ORGANISATIONS ONLY

It is true to say that large organisations are likely to be able to afford high end equipment, services as well as lease lines to get very high levels of quality and reliability. There is nothing to stop a small organisation with a low budget to achieve a high level of quality and service by utilising VOIP. After all, this is what this guide is written for.

As a small organisation, it is often difficult to get a telephone company to install a VOIP system for them. Just think, with only a limited amount of profit in sight, why should a telephone company take a chance when it would be much easier for them to install a standard and well established system.

By installing a standard telephone system, the telephone company can tie the client to using them for all their telephony requirements as all the system components are proprietary. In addition, the telephone company has no control over most of the issues that will affect the quality and reliability of a VOIP system, so why should they risk their reputation and profit by promoting VOIP?

To be brutally honest, most people are not aware of the benefits of VOIP anyway, so for a telephone system supplier, there is no need to do more than is necessary. Since most people will know how a standard telephone system work, what is the point of raising their expectation when it is more profitable and simpler to offer the standard system?

VOIP requires some knowledge of networking including TCP/IP that is traditionally not part of the training of telephone engineers, so a lot of telephone companies will not have the expertise to design and implement VOIP systems. We can see why a lot of telephone system suppliers will try to discourage their clients from considering VOIP.

This guide is written specifically with those potential VOIP users from the smaller organisations in mind. There are so many reasons for implementing VOIP, and I believe, we should always consider it before considering a standard telephone system.

CHAPTER 3

VOIP - WHAT ARE THE ADVANTAGES?

There have been numerous articles and adverts promoting VOIP on websites and magazines etc., there is no point promoting them again here. Instead, we will concentrate on applying VOIP to our scenario to help us make the initial decision.

We will first of all list some of the most common quoted advantages :-

- Low cost implementation
- Low call costs
- flexible (can utilise other available devices and technologies)
- requires fewer or even no telephone lines
- feature rich system with loads of functionality as standard e.g. voicemail etc.
- location independent (remote office and extensions)

Putting ourselves now into Mary's situation, on the surface of it, VOIP seems to tick all the boxes for ACME Ltd. Now let us consider the business needs of the company first. As the company is moving premises, they will need to install either a new system or move their current system to the new premises. Since the current system is deemed to be inadequate even for their current usage, moving it is a non starter. Mary therefore is left with the decision of whether to implement a VOIP solution or a (POTS) plain old telephone system.

As the current system uses ISDN lines, she has to compare the strengths and weaknesses of a conventional ISDN system against a VOIP system. As a small and growing company, she needs to invest wisely. By implementing a system that is flexible and allows for growth as well as rich functionality, she wants to get the biggest return possible for her investment.

WHAT IS GOOD AND BAD ABOUT VOIP?

Before making a decision, Mary decided to go on the internet to do some desk research with regards to the benefits and drawbacks of VOIP. There are countless articles on the internet promoting VOIP and very few against. In particular, VOIP seems to be treated as internet telephony all the time. Very few articles seem to dissociate the VOIP technology itself from the internet. Yet through her research, she has identified that there are lots of products on the market that connects a VOIP system directly to PSTN (Public Switched Telephone Network), ISDN and even GSM (Global System for Mobile communication) for mobile networks. In fact, some of the lower end devices have a facility which is called a lifeline that connects a VOIP system to a standard telephone line enabling calls to be made and received should the internet go down.

This gives Mary an idea, what if her company can actually utilise VOIP for not only internet telephony, but utilise ISDN, analogue lines or even mobile (GSM) too? In her research, she has found nothing to stop her from implementing a system that uses internet telephony, ISDN, Analogue and GSM at the same time. This system should allow her company to benefit from the advantages of both world and hopefully minimises the drawbacks.

The following is a table comparing the relevant strength and weaknesses of both ISDN and VOIP telephone systems (internet telephony). Normal analogue telephone lines (PSTN) is not considered because Mary is not wanting to implement a system that is deemed to be less than her current system with no perceived benefits. Her analogy is based on the assumption that if she is going to implement a standard telephone system and not VOIP, she may as well upgrade her current system and move it rather than pay for a lesser system. After all, she chose the ISDN system over an analogue system at the beginning.

In order to allow her to make a better decision, she wants to look at the advantages and disadvantages of both technologies. She can then try to design a system that can benefit from the best of both technologies. If her calculations are correct, she could help the company implement a low cost, feature rich and reliable telephone system that can offer good quality voice quality.

COMPARISON TABLE ISDN VS VOIP

ISDN	VoIP
Reliability	Reliability dependent on many other factors
High quality	Quality not guaranteed
Does not require external power supply for individual telephones	Requires external power and hence adding extra cabling to the telephones (unless power over Ethernet is used)
High installation costs	Low installation costs
High line costs, number of lines must be physically installed	Complete flexibility in number of channels required
Additional lines in twos (channels) and at high cost	With sufficiently good internet connection, extra channels can be added at low cost
Requires dedicated cabling	Can share computer network cabling
Needs an expensive local PBX	Local PBX at much lower cost
PBX are usually use proprietary technology, requires specialists installation	PBX installation usually through a web interface, can be installed by end user with enough IT skills
Require maintenance charges	Self install, no maintenance charges
Hardware upgrade expensive	Hardware can be upgraded at a lower cost
Limited range of services supported, adding features is very expensive	Massive range of services supported, a lot of features come as standard
Geography defines which numbers are available and how they can be used	VOIP is location independent. Phone calls can be transferred across to other areas over the internet for free. You can select local geographic numbers for almost anywhere

Armed with all these new knowledge and ideas, she decides to step back, take stock and revisit the company business requirements first. She does not want to fall into the trap of implementing VOIP just because it can do lots of cool things. The business requirements must come first.

The business requirements for the new telephone system:-

- simple to install, configure and maintain
- reasonably priced
- feature rich system with telephone logs, voicemail, office closed/ holiday messages, telephone queues and digital receptionists etc.
- good quality calls and reliability
- adequate number of lines with expansion potential
- low cost calls
- integration with remote office and remote workers
- ability to integrate with standard telephone services
- ability to continue operating even when part of the system fails

The next stage is to consider what potential situations could arise that will affect the optimal operation of the new telephone system. They are:-

- power cuts
- failure of the main system PBX
- failure of individual telephones
- internet failure
- standard line failure
- VOIP provider failure

Apart from the reliance on the internet related services (line and VOIP provider), there would have been no difference to having a conventional PBX system. Thinking back, when she was responsible for implementing the current system, there was no consideration to any of the above issues at all. When there was a power cut, everyone just accepted that the telephone system would stop working like all other electrical appliances. If there was a line failure, everyone would expect that they can make no telephone calls outside.

Now that these situations are being considered, the new system must therefore be implemented with the above situations in mind, hopefully, it can address some if not all of them. Having gone through power cuts and line failures without drastic adverse effect to the business, these situations must be considered as minor drawbacks rather than business critical for ACME Ltd. After all, a power cut late in the afternoon in the middle of winter means the office will plunge into darkness anyway, meaningful work cannot really be done by the staff even if they want to continue.

Whilst it is desirable to have the option of being able to make and receive telephone calls even when there is no electricity to the computers, the lights and the heating etc., it is unrealistic to expect the business to continue as normal.

Having said the above, it would definitely be desirable for the business to still be able to receive telephone calls from clients and partners even if only the receptionist can make and answer calls. So provisions must be made so that at least part of the system must remain operational even if there is a power cut.

After careful research and considerations, Mary must now design a logical system that will fulfill all the business requirements of the company. Whether she employs a specialist company to carry out the whole process or to do it all herself, she must come up with a logical system that will work at a realistic price.

CHAPTER 4

THE LOGICAL SYSTEM

Mary's first consideration is to look at all the available telephone call rates to see if she can identify what type of technology is required for the new telephone system. After all, ongoing call costs will more than likely compensate any increase in initial investments. Since the system the company wants should have the capability of making calls by utilising different service providers and different technologies, cost savings should make a higher initial investment worthwhile.

MOBILE CALLS

This is by far the most important and expensive part of the telephone bills since the beginning. Mobile cost accounts for over £4800 of the annual telephone bills. To Mary, all efforts must be made to reduce this. After studying the marketing materials and having made many calls to the sales departments of many telephone companies, she has come to the conclusion that the lowest cost deals available involves using mobile SIM (GSM) pay monthly package. So the new system must be able to utilise mobile SIMs. This has the added benefit that this technology does not require any telephone lines at all, so it will be a good fallback service if the physical lines fail.

Currently, an unlimited monthly package can cost as little as £15 per month, she estimated that the average daily usage for mobile calls for the main office is between 250 to 300 minutes. Assuming most calls are made between 10am to 4pm, over this 6 hour period, the average hourly usage would be between 25 to 35 minutes. In order to cover this requirement, she estimated that she would require a minimum of 2 SIMs to cover the usage. This means that each mobile SIM will be used for between 25 to 35 minutes every hour during this period. Obviously, there may be periods when more than 2 simultaneous call will be made by the staff, but it is expected to be extremely infrequent.

Estimating a monthly cost of say 4 SIM packages for the 2 offices, the monthly mobile bill is expected to be not much more than £70 per month. In comparison, the current month mobile cost of over £450 per month, the potential saving is nearly £5000 per year! According to her rough estimations, this on its own can go a long way in offsetting most or even all of the potential cost of the initial investment. This revenue must be pursued as the highest priority of the system.

INTERNET TELEPHONY

Although this technology requires a reliable and good internet connection, it does not mean that service level must be 100% as it is impossible to achieve anyway. The company currently uses standard ADSL broadband and has experienced nearly no downtime at all in the past year. Within the same period, there was at least 2 serious power cuts which lasted for more than a few minutes in the main office and surrounding district. So the reliability of the internet services should not be a serious issue with the new system. However, it will be prudent to think of an alternative route should the internet service fails.

The new office will benefit from a wireless broadband service provided by a local company. This service is only available as the new office is only 1Km from the service provider and has a clear line of site to the provider's location. The service provides an average 10Mb upstream and 20Mb downstream (upgradable to 40Mb upstream/ 40Mb downstream) which is ideal for remote working as well as VOIP.

The reason for using this wireless broadband service is that the new office is not able to get fibre broadband and is only serviced by normal ADSL at the usual speed. Given that the remote users has always complained about the slow speed when working remotely, this service should provide a noticeable improvement of speed between the two offices as well as for the remote users (the upstream speed of the new service will increase the download speed of the remote office and remote workers).

The alternative to wireless broadband is a lease line, however at 4 times the cost of wireless broadband and roughly the same speed, Mary has decided against it. Just to confirm that the performance is what is quoted, Mary spoke to another wireless broadband client to confirm that the reliability and performance is as good as quoted. As with all broadband, she acknowledges that the speed is not absolutely guaranteed, but the experience of a current user convinces her that the performance is usually around what is expected with very little deviation and the reliability is extremely good. So internet telephony should be part of the new system in add further functionality to the system (certainly for the remote office and remote workers). Remember, calls between offices and remote workers are free as they can be routed over the internet as internal calls. This has a couple of added advantages. Firstly, internal calls do not have to use up a telephone line. Secondly, calls between remote offices and remote users become calls to internal extensions requiring no receptionist to transfer calls or (DDI) direct dial in numbers.

By using a business VOIP communication provider, the company can benefit from unlimited local and national calls as well as low cost international calls too. So internet telephony is a must for the new system if the company wants to integrate the two office telephone system and allow remote users to become part of the telephone system.

STANDARD TELEPHONE LINES
The current system utilises 4 ISDN channels (4 lines) allowing for 4 simultaneous external calls. As the business expands, more and more calls are being made and received, the 4 lines is now proving to be inadequate. Recently, there are more and more occasions where no lines are available for outgoing call as well as external callers complaining they cannot get through.

Mary spoke to the current telephone supplier and discovered that their current telephone system is not upgradable. Although moving this system to the new office is a low cost option, it does not satisfy the business requirements stated before. So a new telephone seems to be inevitable.

As the company requires a reliable telephone service and good quality voice calls, using standard telephone lines makes good sense. The choice is whether to use ISDN or just normal analogue lines, since the implementation cost seems to be very similar, ISDN should be the obvious choice as the call quality should be best.

The biggest attraction for using conventional business lines is that there are many packages available which are great for local and national calls. This includes non geographic numbers like 0845 and 0870 numbers. Mary has been speaking to the sales people of several telephone service suppliers and has found an unlimited call package which only adds a few pounds (under £5) per month to the business. These call packages do not include mobile calls though. But since the new system should be able to make calls to mobiles using SIMs, mobile call costs should not be an issue.

Assuming the new system for the new office will have 4 ISDN lines and two for the remote office , the actual cost of local and national calls will be limited to under £20 per month. This will mean that there is going to be a net saving for local and national calls of over £300 per month. This level of saving is staggering.

Obviously, Mary cannot be blamed for committing the company to using the current service provider as the original business requirements and the original telephone system was quite different. The telephone system has simply evolved and grew with the business into the system it is now and the original telephone provider has not changed because nobody had thought about changing it up till now.

Having looked into call costs and potential savings, it is clear to Mary that the company will require a system with all the features stated in the business requirements section and can utilise the following:-

- link to ISDN lines for quality, reliability and low cost calls
- internet telephony to integrate the two offices and link to remote workers
- use mobile SIMS to make calls to mobile networks
- revert to the ISDN lines should internet fails
- use SIMs and internet telephony should ISDN lines fail
- power supply like a UPS (Uninterruptable Power Supply) to continue operating should there be a power failure

After giving the current telephone provider the business requirements, she was not surprised to receive a quote from them that is many times more than the cost of the current system. After researching the cost and specifications of a VOIP system, it is clear to her that her own design will be much better and will be a fraction of the cost of employing a company to do the project.

Her logical system will consist of a VOIP PBX with the following features:-

- support at least 30 extensions
- support at least 10 concurrent calls
- digital receptionist
- BLF busy lamp field
- call queues
- ring groups
- call logs
- time based rules
- call diversion
- voice conferencing
- voicemail and voicemail to emails

As far as Mary's concerned, for the two offices, she will require two PBXs. In the interest of compatibility, she decides it is best to choose identical devices even if the remote office's requirement is less. In the grand scheme of things, the extra few pounds for one device matters very little.

Whilst all IP PBXs will have the capability of internet telephony, the new PBX must have at least 2 expansion slots, one for ISDN connections with at least 2 BRI (basic rate interface) ports, this will support 4 voice channels (lines) and one for installation of 2 SIM cards. This PBX should allow the telephone system to utilise landlines, internet as will as SIMs.

Besides the PBX , she will require business quality industry standard SIP telephones. Since most of the work of the telephone system is done by the PBX, the SIP phones should be simple to operate and functionality can be sacrificed for simplicity and reliability. The only exceptions will be the two reception phones as they need to do a bit more e.g. BLF to indicate whether an extension is available, engaged or off line altogether. The SIP phones must also have 2 network ports in order to allow the phones to act as a switch to link the local area network socket to the staff's PC. This will reduce the number of cables and sockets required for the new office network, hence significantly lowering the cabling installation cost.

FOR MAIN OFFICE

In order to keep the telephone system running even during a power cut, UPSs are necessary to supply electricity to crucial components of the system. The company currently uses a UPS for their server already , so Mary is quite familiar with how they work.

The components that needs to keep operating are:-

- the PBX
- internet router
- 24 port switch that links all the devices on the LAN together
- reception PC and SIP phone for reception

Currently, the 24 port switch is plugged into the UPS together with the server, past power cuts has shown that the UPS can only keep the server and switch operating for around 20 minutes or so, Mary decided it would be wise to use separate UPS for the internet router and the switch since they use much less electricity and should last much longer on a separate UPS. Finally for the reception PC and SIP phone, Mary thinks one UPS should be sufficient.

The 3 UPSs are designed to keep the system going for at least 20 minutes. The thinking behind this configuration is that most power cuts only last 5 to 10 minutes, so the anticipated 20 minutes should cover most power cuts. In the event of a power cut lasting a lot longer, the hope is that by the time the server is gracefully powered off, the reception PC will be switched off as well by the receptionist, leaving the UPS to supply only the reception phone.

FOR REMOTE OFFICE

The remote office will also require UPS for the reception PC and SIP phone. As the remote office has no server, Mary decided that one UPS should be enough to support the internet router, PBX, small 8 port switch, the reception PC and the reception SIP phone.

Whilst it is important to think about the ability to continue operating during a power cut, other circumstances may make the backup plan irrelevant anyway. As mentioned earlier, if the power cut is during late afternoon in winter, the darkness will make any attempt to work almost impossible. In addition, without the use of computers, there will not be much useful work done since there will be no emails and no way of accessing and saving data. So the main objective for the UPS backup strategy is to allow reception to continue receiving calls and taking messages etc. for as long as possible.

CABLING

Mary has also looked into the network cabling too, although any standard (CAT5) cable will do for standard desktop computers (they do not often get moved), it is not the same for a SIP phone. The back of each SIP phone will have three cables plugged into it, if the network cabling used is thick and hard, it will be very awkward to position the SIP phone in a suitable spot on the desk. If like most people, the telephone gets moved regularly to create space or out of the way temporarily, the network plug can be accidently dislodged from the socket at the back, causing the phone to malfunction. So the company will be looking at using thin/flat and flexible cables for the SIP phones.

DUPLICATE COMPONENTS

After looking at the cost of components, Mary has the idea that she can keep a spare (identical) component for everything that is crucial. A spare 24 port switch, a spare reception SIP phone and even a spare PBX if the price is within reason. Keeping spare parts means failed crucial components can be replaced almost as soon as they are identified. This will mean a much quicker fix than calling the telephone engineer. After all, it is not that difficult to replace them by unplugging everything and plugging everything back in after replacement. The main thing is, she needs to know how to configure the PBX and the SIP phones. If she knows how to install the whole system, she will know how to replace all the components too.

Having visited the websites of a few providers, Mary decided the only way to find out is to actually put them to the test. Her logic is to buy a low cost SIP phone, subscribe to a few providers and just try them out. One provider even provides a free trial subscription which will allow her to try the quality and review their features. With a low cost SIP phone, she can evaluate how well they can work. The assumption is that with a cheap SIP phone and a standard broadband connection with no quality of service configuration, the tests should show up how bad internet telephony can be.

After trying several well known providers, she was pleasantly surprised to find that all of them provided good quality calls and in most cases, the person she called was not even aware that she was using internet telephony. All her test calls are made to local and national numbers, she is not expecting the company to have a requirement for making international calls at all, so no calls overseas were tried.

She is now confident that under normal operating conditions, a VOIP telephone system should perform as well as a standard system in terms of call quality. All she needs to do is to ensure that external influences are minimised and reliability is provisioned.

The new telephone system will logically work like this:-

FOR MAIN OFFICE
- 4 ISDN lines in the new office
- subscription to unlimited local and national package with ISDN line provider
- subscription to a reliable VOIP provider
- *SIP trunk with the capacity for several simultaneous calls
- subscription to unlimited local and national call package with VOIP provider
- PBX with ISDN ports and SIM slots

- PBX connected to ISDN lines
- PBX connected to the VOIP provider
- two SIMs installed and working in the PBX
- SIP phones for all users
- pre-configured spare reception phone and spare PBX
- permanent call forwarding (extra cost) of ISDN number to the VOIP provider
- PBX to register with VOIP provider to receive all incoming calls
- VOIP provider service configured to forward all calls to ISDN number should internet fails at main office
- dial rules created including rules for landline and mobile calls via ISDN lines or SIMs
- SIP trunk (connection between two VOIP systems) created between the two offices to allow calls to extensions in other office over the internet
- mobile app for remote staff to allow their mobiles to become extensions
- all staff trained to use the system efficiently

For the remote office, the plan is identical with the exception of the number of ISDN lines and the number of extensions

HOW THE SYSTEM SHOULD WORK
ISDN lines
The main reasons for using ISDN lines is consistent good call quality and reliability. Because ISDN is not affected by internet network conditions, the quality of calls can be more or less maintained consistently and reliably just like a normal non VOIP based system. By subscribing to a monthly package with unlimited calls which includes all local, national and some non-geographical numbers, the call charges can be minimised.

The ISDN lines can be expected to work reliably even if internet service has failed as it does not rely on the internet at all, so it can be the back bone of the system. By forwarding all incoming calls to the company to the VOIP provider, this will effectively allow the 4 ISDN lines to be outgoing only lines. As such, the staff can expect consistently good quality outgoing calls.

The strategy of using ISDN is only a temporary measure, in the long run, the idea would be to move both incoming and outgoing calls to internet telephony. Of course, it will be subjected to call quality and reliability being consistently maintained. A period of 12 months to 18 months has been set for this long term test. As the strategy of using ISDN can be permanent one, the company is not going to lose any level of required service or system reliability by sticking with it should internet telephony proves to be not satisfactory in the new office location. Remember, some environment may make internet telephone unsuitable for constant use e.g. poor or unreliable internet service. Unfortunately, only time will tell and the company is not wanting to start off trialling a system without knowing its quality from the start. After a site survey, the wireless broadband supplier confirms that the new office will benefit from a very reliable and high speed internet connection. So the slight risk of unknown service quality for a small part (incoming calls) is considered to be worth taking.

USING INTERNET TELEPHONY

The VOIP system will utilise the wireless broadband for all incoming calls and as a backup for outgoing calls should the ISDN lines fail.

As incoming calls are less frequent than outgoing calls, Mary is prepared to use the SIP trunk for all incoming calls. With only one and occasionally two simultaneous incoming calls, the bandwidth required should not be very high, so call quality is expected to be good under normal operating conditions as proven with her trials with standard broadband. After the site survey that confirms the availability of good and reliable service, the decision of using internet telephony is considered to be sound.

Potentially, a second internet connection (standard ADSL) as a fall back was considered. The idea would be to switch to standard broadband for incoming calls should the main wireless broadband service fails. However, this idea was rejected as the VOIP provider's system can be configured to automatically forward all calls back to the ISDN lines if the internet service fails (VOIP system fails to register with the VOIP service providers SIP server). So there will be no need to manually configure an alternative since the system can already do it automatically. A second internet (standard ADSL) must be available if the company switches to complete internet telephony for all incoming calls so there will be no ISDN lines to switch back to.

MOBILE CALLS

The new VOIP system will have the capability of allowing at least 2 SIM cards to be installed. This effectively allows for 2 simultaneous calls to mobile networks by using the SIMs to cut cost to mobile networks. Theoretically, the SIMs can also be used if ISDN and internet telephony services have both failed simultaneously. However, this situation is not expected and cannot be considered to be a realistic backup.

Since not all mobile networks offer the same quality of service everywhere, the mobile network operators will be chosen after trials. The company has decided to use 2 different mobile operators for the 2 SIMS, in the hope that it is unlikely for 2 different providers service to fail at the same time.

A cheap and effective way to test mobile call quality is to purchase a Pay As You Go package from 2 or 3 providers and test the reception strength and the call quality and reception with mobile phones. A possible way to choose the most appropriate mobile network is by using the internet to search for the providers masts closest to the new location. By going to the website http://sitefinder.ofcom.org.uk/, the various mobile network operator masts locations can be identified. By choosing the operators with masts that are closest to the new office location, it is likely they will offer the best quality of service.

With mobile calls, it is impossible to guarantee highest possible call quality all the time because there is no control over where the recipient of a call will be. If the person called is on a train travelling through a tunnel, the quality of the call will very likely be extremely poor if it worked at all. So for the purpose of choosing a mobile network operator, call quality can only be judged by normal calling conditions e.g. in an office or a house etc.

The logical system should work as show in the diagram below:-

DIAGRAM SHOWING HOW THE NEW VOIP SYSTEM SHOULD WORK

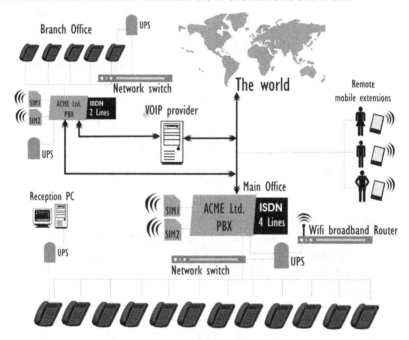

SUMMARY

The company is going to implement a new telephone system that is based on VOIP. The new system will be low cost and simple to install, feature rich, reliable in operation and offers least cost routing of calls to minimise call cost. In comparison to a conventional telephone system, it will cost a fraction of the initial cost to implement and the running cost including call cost and maintenance will be a fraction of a conventional system too.

On the other hand, there are a few issues the company must take into account. Firstly, since the system is not going to be purchase from one single service provider as a whole operational system, the responsibility will fall upon Mary to ensure that it is correctly planned, installed and operated. Should things go wrong for any reason, there will be no other company to shoulder the blame.

Since Mary will be designing the system herself, the company must depend on Mary alone to be correct with her judgements. The system itself will be unique, a lot of the components will not be tested until they are actually in place. Compatibility issues may arise as the components may not be designed to work together efficiently, Mary can only rely upon the specifications provided by the vendors. At best, she can only rely on the technical support of the vendors to provide help.

There are other issues that cannot be evaluated fully without actually putting the system on line for testing. For example, until the PBX is fully installed and connected to all the services like ISDN lines, VOIP providers and SIMs, there will be no way of assessing the call qualities - "crystal clear voice quality" quoted in the brochure provided by the vendor is no guarantee of good call quality and must not be taken at face value. The second issue is how well and reliable is the internet connection and service of the VOIP provider? Until the system is on line, there is no way of knowing the answer.

With the potential savings of many thousands of pounds and backups fully considered, the company has decided to go ahead with VOIP and Mary is finally given the task to design, install and be fully in charge of the whole project.

CHAPTER 5

THE PHYSICAL SYSTEM

Now that the logical system has been designed, the next step is to plan a physical system. This will be the actual system that will physically be put into place and will operate for real.

The most important component of the VOIP system is the PBX. The PBX can be either a software that runs on a computer or an appliance. In simple terms, a PBX does the job of a telephone exchange operator in the early days of telephony. The basic functions of a PBX are:-

- to connect all the telephone extensions to a physical device (branch exchange) within the location
- enable these extensions to make calls to each other
- enable all calls from extensions to be made to the outside world and vice versa

A VOIP PBX, commonly called a SIP server, has a lot of extra features pre-programmed as part of its software as standard. In most cases, these software can be managed and configured by a web user interface which makes it much easier for non telephone specialists like Mary to operate it. Some of these extra features are:-

- voicemail including voicemail to email
- least cost routing
- ability to connect to ISDN lines, mobile operators via SIMs, internet telephony
- linking more than one office PBX together to allow for inter-office calls over the internet
- mobile extensions for remote users to be part of the system by using apps on their smart phones
- remote users operating from home can be part of the system
- detailed call logs
- digital receptionists
- IVR interactive voice response
- call queues

- time based rules
- music on hold
- caller id
- voice conferencing
- busy lamp field
- ring group
- speed dial

It is sometimes possible to add these features to standard PBX based systems, but it will usually incurred a high cost.

THE CHOICES

There are numerous products on the market that are all capable of offering all or some of the features required by the company.

HOSTED SERVICE

One service that is promoted by a lot of the telephone service providers nowadays is hosted service. By using a hosted service, the company can have most of the features above without even needing a local PBX.

This eliminates the necessity of knowing how to install and configure a device that can be a bit tricky. In addition, the PBX will be maintained by specialists with much higher grade equipment.

The only requirement for the company is for all users to configure their SIP phones to use the hosted service. All available features can be configured via a fairly simple web user interface.

This would have been a great service for the company if it is not for the following issues:-

- dependence on the internet - reliability and quality is subjected to condition outside the control of the company
- no lease cost routing - the company spends a lot on calls, using a hosted service means routing all calls through on provider
- dependence on one provider - there is no quick and easy way to test the service quality of the service provider beforehand, it is very difficult to change provider after the system is implemented should things not work out

After taking the pros and cons into account, Mary decided to not use a hosted service. Her decision is based on the fact that the company needs to have the flexibility of routing calls through different service providers. The company also needs to have the comfort of knowing it can depend on a reliable and good quality service and a back up service should the main service fail.

Finally, to configure a hosted service for all the users will be equivalent to doing most of the work of installing a local SIP server for the company anyway. The only difference is that the hosted SIP server is configured over the internet. The requirement for routing mobile calls via the SIMs and ISDN lines means a local PBX is required, so a hosted service merely duplicates some of the work and makes no sense.

Software PBX (SIP Servers)

There are many SIP server software available on the market, they range from open source free software like the very popular Asterisk™ based on Linux to the Microsoft Windows™ based 3CX for Windows ™ that is a payable commercial product.

Option 1 - Windows based Software PBX (3CX for Windows)

Looking at the various versions of 3CX products, it is obviously very appealing to the Mary as it is Windows based, this implies it is simple to install. As she is already managing the company's Windows based server, she is confident that installing 3CX would be fairly simple.

After studying the features of the various versions of 3CX, she can see that all the requirements of the company can be met. A free (cut down) version is available for downloading from the vender's site, so she will have the opportunity to try it first.

The installation of the trial package is fairly simple and Mary managed to test the product by using one of the company's trial VOIP providers. The call quality was as good as using a standalone SIP phone and more than adequate for the company's requirements.

In order to operate 3CX PBX for Windows, the company requires extra devices to link it to PSTN lines and mobile networks. They are as follows:-

- a computer to act run the software
- ISDN BRI gateway to connect to the ISDN lines
- VOIP GSM gateway to connect to mobile networks

It is not satisfactory to use any old desktop or laptop computer to run 3CX PBX for Windows as the VOIP system is required to run 24/7 and 7 days a week. So Mary will be looking at using the current company server to run the software which may add more uncertainties to the operation and reliability of the VOIP system, not to mention potential issues with the server having to run extra software.

If the company invests into purchasing a computer that is rated to run 24/7, then it will add substantially to the cost of the implementation.

THE SERVER

The server considered is the Dell Power Edge TII, this is one of the most basic servers on the market. The company is not looking for a super fast server as it is only interested in the reliability of the system that is required to run the VOIP server software. The specification is as follows:-

- Intel® Core™ Processor i3-2120, 2C/4T, 3.30GHz, 3M Cache, 65W TDP
- 4GB RAM
- 500GB hard drive
- DVD drive
- Windows Server 2012, Essentials Edition, Factory Installed
  The estimated cost is £650 + VAT and shipping

Ideally, the server should have a RAID 1 (mirrored drives) for extra reliability. Mirrored drives allow for one drive failure without the system going down, but this configuration does not support the hardware and operating system. The server can operate and be managed by remote desktop without the need of a monitor, keyboard and mouse after the initial setup, so they were not included in the costing.

ISDN BRI GATEWAY

After having researched into the various potential ISDN gateways, Mary decided to look into the Patton range of products. The Patton Smartnode™ 4120 appears to fit the bill as it is supported by most of the industry standard VOIP systems including 3CX, Asterisk etc. and should to be worth considering as the gateway to link the new VOIP system to make landline calls. It supports 4 simultaneous calls, so it satisfies the minimum requirements at least. The estimated price for this unit is £320 + VAT and shipping

VOIP GSM GATEWAY

The Portech MV372 can accommodate 2 SIMs and allows for 2 simultaneous calls. It can both make calls to and receive calls from other mobile networks as well as landlines. This satisfies the minimum requirements of the company.
The estimated price is £335 +VAT and shipping.

UPS (UNINTERRUPTABLE POWER SUPPLY)

The APC BE550G-UK is a relatively low cost unit, allowing for low power systems to continue operating for a short period of time. The main aim of the company is to allow the VOIP system to operate for a few extra minutes in the hope that power will come back up within a few minutes. At least, the company is wanting the system to shut down gracefully to prevent issues on restart when power comes back on.
The cost of these units are about £60 + VAT and delivery each.

The company recognises that there is a limit to how long the UPS can continue to operate in the event of a power cut. Their experience is that the battery of these units will operate for around 20 minutes after loss of power. This assumes it is powering a standard type PC, it will last much longer for low power devices like switches and routers.

DIAGRAM SHOWING HOW THE PHYSICAL SYSTEM WOULD WORK WITH 3CX FOR WINDOWS

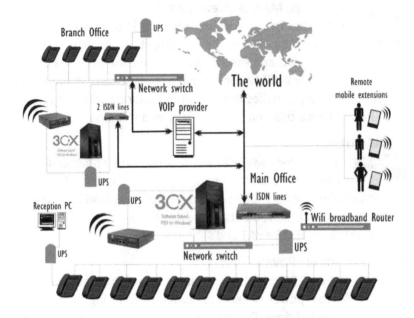

SUMMARY FOR OPTION1

The most obvious considerations with regards to using 3CX are the requirement for 2 reliable computers and operating system licences as well as the licences for the 3CX software. The list of total requirements for the VOIP system are listed below:-

- 2 x server class computers and operating system software
- 3CX licence for main office (8 simultaneous calls)
- 3CX licence for remote office (4 simultaneous calls)
- 2 x Patton Smartnode 4120
- 2 x Portech MV372

The estimated rough costs of this system for comparative purposes are :-

2 X servers at £650 each £1300

2 X Sip server licences £800

2 X Patton Smartnode 4120 at £320 each £640

2 X Portech MV372 at £335 each £670

4 X APC UPS at £60 each £240

Total cost without taking VAT and delivery into account............£3650

The advantages of the 3CX system are:-

- Microsoft Windows based and Mary is familiar with the operating system
- low cost in comparison to a conventional telephone system
- SIP servers can be utilised for other tasks such as fax services
- reasonably simple to configure
- support supplied by local dealers (at extra cost)
- feature rich
- very powerful system allowing for expansion

On the other hand, there are disadvantages too, they are:

- requirement of expensive computers as servers
- licensing of the software for the 2 office systems
- requirement of extra hardware devices like the Patton and Portech
- more individual devices to connect to system means more configuration and more to go wrong
- high cost of these devices

As the company is not looking to expand rapidly in the foreseeable future, there is not really a need for such a powerful system, so Mary decided to just use the 3CX system as a reference system for comparison purposes only.

OPTION 2 - OPEN SOURCE SOFTWARE PBX (ASTERISK)

Asterisk is an open source development project, it is stable, reliable and is used by thousands of systems worldwide. Most important of all, it is free. This means that some of the software sip servers based on Asterisk e.g. FreePBX can be obtained free of charge and they are supported by forums whose members have published a lot of solutions to most issues one may encounter regarding Asterisk configuration and operation.

Alternatively, there are paid support services e.g. UK based Services for Asterisk that offer paid support, this means the users are not left on their own device when facing technical issues.

DIAGRAM SHOWING HOW THE PHYSICAL SYSTEM WOULD WORK WITH ASTERISK BASED PBX

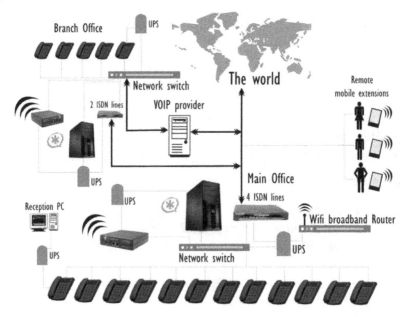

Looking at this system, it is obvious that there is very little difference between the operation, configuration and the cost of the software based SIP servers. The only difference is the cost of the licenses for 3CX and the Microsoft server operating system while the Asterisk based software is free.

The estimated total cost of the hardware is estimated to be around £1000 less because there will be no licensing cost of PBX software and the operating system.

SUMMARY FOR OPTION 2

Taking the cost of support into account, there may not be a great deal of difference between the 2 solutions after all.

OPTION 3 - PBX APPLIANCE (ZYCOO COOVOX U50)

PBX appliances

The two SIP server solutions above are based on very powerful computers to operate the VOIP system. With less than a couple of dozen users spreading over 2 office sites plus a handful of remote users, it is possible to consider dedicated devices that are much less powerful but designed to do operate as PBX only appliances.

There is a wide range of these appliances on the market manufacture by many different vendors. However, they are usually just very small computers running some versions of the very popular Asterisk software with a web user interface.

After spending some time on the specifications of the various appliances, Mary decided on the Zycoo CooVox U50.

THE ZYCOO COOVOX U50

Unlike the other options, the U50 comes in the form of a small box not much bigger than some internet routers. It is capable of having up to 2 modules installed to give it extra capabilities that the company requires.

2 X GSM MODULE

This module can accept up to 2 standard SIMs from one or two mobile operators. Once the SIMs are installed, the module can then be installed into one of the 2 available slots on the U50. This will allow extensions from this system to make calls to mobile or landlines through one of the two available SIMs.

---

4 BRI MODULE

This module allows the U50 to be connected to 4 ISDN lines and therefore allows the system to make up to 8 simultaneous calls by using these ISDN lines.

With the addition of these 2 modules, the U50 will have all the functionality required by the company and the cost is significantly lower than the other options.

The total price of the U50 including the GSM and BRI modules is around £410 + VAT and delivery.

DIAGRAM SHOWING HOW THE PHYSICAL SYSTEM WOULD WORK WITH ZYCOO U50 PBX APPLIANCE

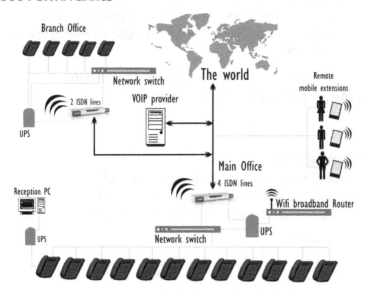

SUMMARY OF OPTION 3

Looking at the diagram, it is obvious that a VOIP system based on the U50 is much simpler and of course, the total cost of implementation appears to be less. The list of required equipment are :-

2 X Zycoo U50 ....£410

2 X GSM modules 2 SIM versions £230

2 X ISDN BRI modules £190

3 X UPS...£180

The total cost of these equipment comes to around £1010 + VAT and delivery.

The advantages of the U50 based VOIP system over the other options are:-

- low cost at less than half the cost of even the Asterisk system
- the extra modules are guaranteed to work with the PBX
- simpler system hence simpler configuration
- uses a lot less power
- reliability as there are no moving parts like hard drives etc.
- less connected devices like the extra gateways means there is less to go wrong

The disadvantages are:-

- total failure if an appliance fails
- close system with few upgrade paths
- appliance designed for small organisations limited to no more than 20 simultaneous calls

From the point of view of Mary, the disadvantages are not really that important. The same argument for complete failure can be applied to the previous two options too, if the computer that runs the SIP server software fails the whole system will fail as well. Since the company is not expected to grow significantly in the near future, no substantial upgrade is necessary.

With a standard 4 port BRI module (subject to having 4 ISDN lines), the U50 can support up to 8 simultaneous calls which is double that of the current requirement. In addition, the 2X SIM module can be replaced by a 4XSIM module to support 4 simultaneous mobile calls.

So in conclusion, this option represents the lowest cost in terms of initial implementation and the running cost will be as low as any of the other 2 options. The decision is therefore to implement a new VOIP system based on the Zycoo U50.

CHAPTER 6

THE TRIAL

One big advantage of implementing a low cost device like the U50 is that you can actually run a trial of the actual system at low cost first. Implementation of a conventional or VOIP system using an external provider would entail the commitment to the project with no way of turning back even if the system does not eventually work to the satisfaction of the company.

The company therefore decides to carry out a trial with half a dozen users on one system first. The main objectives of this trial are:-

- quality of calls over the internet
- quality of internal calls
- voice to email operation
- call quality of mobile extensions
- call quality of remote extensions
- use of call queues
- use of music on hold
- use of ring groups
- use of BLF lights to monitor extension status
- use of time based rules
- use of call conferencing

Apart from the quality of calls and voicemail via emails, all the rest of the list above are for interest only and are not crucial to whether the system is going to be implemented.

First of all, the company must established trial accounts with various service providers in order to test the call qualities of their services.

VOIP PROVIDERS
Voipfone- www.voipfone.co.uk

This company offers a full range of IP telephony services. For testing purposes, it is possible to purchase a 500 minute package for £4.75 + VAT. For quality testing purpose, it should be adequate.

Draytel - www.draytel.org

This company offers a full range of IP telephony services. For testing purposes, it is possible to pay for their silver tariff service which costs £20 + VAT. This amount is used to purchase call credits of up to £20 + VAT, this includes a local number. If the company decides to continue using this number and services, they can do so by keeping the account active and in credit.

Soho66 - www.soho66.co.uk

This company offers a full range of IP telephony services. For testing purposes, a single user VOIP package for £3.95 + VAT per month is available and call credits can be purchased separately. Since this package is a monthly plan, it has to be cancelled if the company does not wish to continue using them. Once again, a local geographical number is included.

After setting up trial accounts with the above companies, the next stage is to order the hardware. Apart from the Zycoo U50, Mary decided to purchase half a dozen SIP phones for trial purposes to see well they work.

The company has always believed that it is not necessary to purchase the most expensive gear, however, the equipment purchased must be good enough quality and good for the purpose. Without knowing how good the SIP phones are, the only way is to try several makes and models and put them to the test for real. After looking at the websites of several suppliers, Mary decided to go for the phones with the best functions and of course, at the lowest cost.

In order to save on cabling cost, all SIP phones must have dual network sockets. This will allow for the phone to be connected to the local area network and act as a link to connect the PC to the LAN at the same time. However, this means the SIP phone must be on in order to allow the PC to remain connected to the LAN. This also limits the speed of the network connection to the speed of the Sip phone's network speed - in this case 100MBit. Since the company's software and hardware does not require very high speed links, this does not pose an issue with the operation of the LAN.

Reception phone
Grandstream GXP2160 (£80 + VAT)

This phone is designed for general reception purposes. It is capable of having up to 6 SIP accounts and has up to 24 dual coloured BLF (busy lamp field) keys which are programmable. This phone will be used purely by reception for taking incoming calls from different accounts/lines and to transfer calls to internal extensions. The BLF lights can also be used to monitor the online status of extensions which may be useful.

Grandstream GXP1450 (£45 + VAT and delivery)

This phone is designed for extension users as they only need to make, receive and transfer calls. No other functions are expected to be required. For the trial, the company is interested in the quality of calls and how well it operates.

Yealink T20 (£55 + VAT and delivery)

Just like the Grandstream GXP1450, the trial is to establish if this range of phones are better than the Grandstream or Polycom in terms of call and build quality.

Polycom SoundPoint IP 331 (£90 + VAT and delivery Polycom 456)

This is the most expensive of all the phones to be used for the trial, the company is interested in finding out if is significantly better than the rest.

Grandstream Wave (Free App)

Grandstream Wave is a mobile app that runs on Android smart phones, just like any softphone for VOIP, it enables the user's smart phone to become an extension to a VOIP system. The software utilises either 3G or WIFI to connect to the company's PBX and allow the extension user to make and receive calls as part of the local system.

Before opening the boxes and starting to play with the equipment, a plan must be created to ensure the company's requirements are met.

SECURITY FOR THE SYSTEM

It is common knowledge that the default port used by SIP (5060) is vulnerable to hacker attacks, so an alternative port must be used. Obviously, common default ports like port 25 (smtp - simple mail transfer protocol) or port 110 (pop3 - post office protocol 3) should not be used as they may conflict with other applications. A randomly chosen port number 7655 is chosen as the port that remote extensions and remote office can use to connect to the main office.

Passwords is another important issue to consider, easy to guess passwords that are defaults for various equipment must be changed. In particular, the Zycoo CoooVox U50's administrators password must be strong, so "%_A6m3lTd" was chosen, from now on the administrators password will be referred to as " admin password".

Individual SIP phones can be managed via a web interface. Since it may be necessary to work on these extensions quite regularly, it was decided to configure usernames and passwords for each phone by using part of their extensions. Using the extension number as the username and password would be very easy to remember, but it is very weak and easy to guess. So for usernames, the policy will be the "99" plus the extension number. The password will be the extension number where "Z" will be used to replace the number 2 (the first number of all the extensions) and a "mE" will be added to the end, so extension 201 will have a username of "99201" and password of "Z01mE". This will allow Mary to easily work out the username and passwords for every extension without having to use weak passwords like the actual extension numbers.

For the extension users to access their voicemail (if necessary) by their PIN, a "9" is added to the beginning of the extension and a "5" is added to the end. So the voicemail PIN for extension 201 will be "92015". The reason for using pure numbers is that it is much easier to dial numbers with the keypad of the phones.

For mobile app extensions, the username will be the first name of the user, the password will follow the same convention as the standard. So for example, Peter uses his smart phone as an extension. Let's say he is assigned with an extension of 261, his username for his extension will be "peter" and the password will be "$Z61mE". The reason for not using the standard rule for the username is just in case the smart phone gets stolen, the different settings makes it less easy to guess the usernames of the system in general.

For the individual SIP Phones, the password should also be changed to something that is not easy to guess. It was decided that the password will be "aCmeltd" for all SIP Phones.

Whilst the above username and password policy is by no means fool proof, it will mean that the VOIP system will be implemented with no factory set security, so any would be hacker will not be able to hack into the system by relying on the default values set by the manufacturers. The fact that there is a simple rule for usernames and passwords means working them out is simple.

Some staff commented that it is lot of consideration for very little and the only benefit of hacking into the system is that they will be able to make free calls. Mary's argument is that it takes next to no extra effort to add an extra few characters to any of the settings, but it will discourage the would be attackers.

EXTENSION NUMBERS

Extension number range for main office as well as the remote office will remain the same. So staff will not have to remember who is at what extension again. The current range of extensions at the main office starts at 201 and the remote office starts at 601.

VOICEMAIL

All staff will have voicemail enabled and all voicemails will be sent via emails to the inbox of all the staff. Although a copy is kept on the PBX until deleted. It is expected that once the process has been established and working reliably, the voicemails will be sent via emails only and deleted after it has been sent. The advantage of voicemail emails is that they can be kept and stored in a relevant location in the file system. The company is a bit concerned about the reliability of voicemail via email, so in order to eliminate the yellow sticky note process, they will need something proven to be more reliable. The truth is, the main reason for wanting voicemail via email is that the yellow sticky note process has been extremely unreliable to begin with!

Call flow

DIAGRAM SHOWING THE CURRENT CALL FLOW FOR MAIN OFFICE

All incoming calls

Main Office

Receptionist

Internal extensions

Secretary   non admin staff

Currently at the main office, all incoming calls are answered by the receptionist or whoever is at the reception desk. If the call is not answered in 20 seconds, then it will be forwarded to two of the secretaries. However, due to reorganisation, one of the secretary's room has been taken over by other staff members, so all these incoming calls end up with one secretary. If the secretary is not available, one of the other staff members will have to answer them. Although it is not a very common occurrence, these staff members are not too happy to either answer the calls or having to listen to the phone ringing frequently. Since the flow has been programmed into the system and nobody knows how to change it, the call flow remains and is viewed as a minor nuisance by some staff.

As part of the trial, the company will try ring groups and call queues to evaluate the options and find out which is the best solution.

Ring Groups

With ring groups, the idea is for all incoming calls to be answered by the receptionist or whoever is in the receptionist group (to be decided as the trial progresses).

DIAGRAM SHOWING THE RING GROUP PROCESS FOR MAIN OFFICE

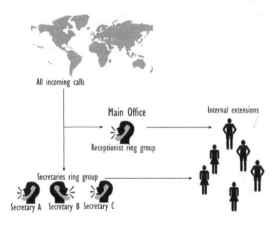

If the receptionist is already on a call, the incoming call will be immediately diverted to the secretaries ring group. Secretary A will be the main person allocated to receive incoming calls if the receptionist is engaged or not available. The flow will continue to the next secretary and so on.

There is a weakness to this process pointed out by the receptionist. If the receptionist is not at her desk, the caller will have to wait at least an extra 20 seconds before the call is being answered. If the appointed secretary is also not available, the waiting time will be even longer.

An alternative is to make all secretary group's extension ring simultaneously if the receptionist is not available, however, this will mean the other secretaries may have to answer more calls than necessary.

Knowing what the potential weaknesses of this call flow, the trial for this process will have the objective of seeing whether this is a significantly better call flow than the current one.

CALL QUEUE

The management thinks that a call queue may make the company appear more professional and allows for a better call process. In this scenario, all calls will be answered by the queue immediately, the receptionist's extension will be the only one that rings. An announcement will welcome the caller followed by background music if the call is not being picked up. The caller will wait until the receptionist answers the call.

Diagram showing the call queue process for Main Office

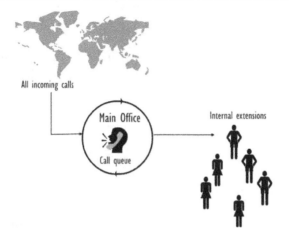

The potential weaknesses of this process is that immaterial of whether the receptionist is available or not, the caller will be subjected to listening to at least part of a recorded message which may not be well received. And since the receptionist will be solely responsible for answering all incoming calls, there may be pressure for her to complete all calls very quickly.

One proposal is to nominate certain secretaries to be the quick response backups. This means that if the caller wants to leave a message to a person and not a voicemail, the secretary can take over from the receptionist, leaving the receptionist to answer the next call.

After all the considerations and planning, it is now time to put the system through its paces. In order to do so, Mary created a list of tasks that she thinks will allow the company to properly assess the system.

Task List
- order equipment
- subscription to the VOIP providers
- create on hold music and voice over
- nominate secretaries for quick response

- nominate secretaries for the ring groups
- nominate test users
- create time based rules for office open and office closed

All users are given a notepad to note down any errors plus issues that they think may be worth considering in order to improve the final system.

CHAPTER 7

PUTTING THE PLAN INTO ACTION

The most important thing to do first is to log into the U50 to change and configure it so that it becomes part of the LAN. The unit comes preconfigured to use the default "Class C" private address of 192.168.1.100 and port 9999 is assigned for web access. This means that the web user interface can be accessed by using 192.168.1.100:9999 to access the U50.

Unfortunately, the current ip address for the LAN is 192.168.6. xxx, which means that the U50 cannot be accessed by any PC on the current network. This is because the address of 192.168.1.100 is on a different network signified by the octet 1 (the number 1 within the U50's default address). The simplest way of accessing the U50 to reconfigure it is to changed the ip address of one of the PCs on the LAN from acquiring settings automatically (DHCP) to a static assignment of something like 192.168.1.10 in order to be within the same network as the U50.

Once the chosen PC's ip address has been changed to be within the same network as the U50, the PC will then be able to access the user interface of the U50. Obviously, the ip address of the U50 will then need to be changed to be in the same network as the LAN. So 192.168.6.100 is chosen as it is easy to remember and this address does not conflict with the DHCP (currently from 192.168.6.150 - 250) range and any devices with fixed ip address on the network.

CREATING EXTENSIONS

For the trial, 6 SIP phones are available. The reception GXP 2160 will be allocated as extension 201, one GXP 1450 will be allocated a remote extension and it will be extension 261 which will be used by one of the home based staff. The other 4 SIP phones will be allocated 202, 203, 204 and 205. Grandstream Wave is downloaded from the Google Apps Store. and the extension for the mobile user will be 301.The convention of passwords, voicemail passwords etc. will be as defined in chapter 6.

CREATING SIP TRUNKS TO THE 3 VOIP PROVIDERS

The process of creating a SIP trunk to a provider is more or less the same as configuring a SIP phone to the provider. You will need the following:-

- Hostname of the SIP servers - sip.voipfone.net, draytel.org and sip.soho66.co.uk
- port or proxy port number - usually not required
- username or account name and passwords for each account

Once the U50 is configured to register to these providers correctly, calls can then be made and received through it.

CONFIGURING THE FIREWALL

For security reasons described and defined in chapter 6, the router will be configured to port forward from port 7655 UDP (user datagram protocol) to 5060 (UDP) of the U50 at 192.168.6.100. This effectively means the router will open port 7655 and not port 5060 to allow UDP traffic used by VOIP to be forwarded to port 5060 of the U50.

CREATING THE TIME BASED RULES

The Main office is open Monday to Friday between 9.00am to 5.00pm. For the initial trial, the system will be set to answer all calls by the receptionist during opening hours. Based on the ring group plan specified in chapter 6, if the receptionist is already on a call the caller will be forwarded to the secretary ring group. A caller will also be forwarded to the secretary ring group if the receptionist is not available, this will happen if the reception extension is not answered within 20 seconds. This means that all incoming calls should be answered by either the receptionist or one of the secretaries.

A second trial will be based on the use of a queuing system as planned in chapter 6. In this scenario, all incoming calls will be answered by the receptionist and will be transferred to the right extension or to the nominated secretary within a minute or so. It is hoped that this should cover all incoming calls during office hours as long as the reception is manned all the time.

OUT OF OFFICE HOURS

The plan is to play an out of hours message at 5.00pm until the next morning at just before 9.00am during the week. The same message will be played all day Saturday and Sunday. The caller will be given the option to leave a voice message after the out of hours message. The voicemail messages will be emailed to Mary who will forward these voicemails to the right staff.

CREATING THE ON HOLD MUSIC AND VOICEOVERS

The company decides to create all the voiceovers and use copyright free music for their VOIP system. The management likes the idea of some sort of marketing message to be included while callers are waiting.

There are loads of music available for use with the VOIP PBXs, some are free and some not. There are professionally created music specifically designed for on hold music at a price to suit any requirements. They also come in different formats e.g. MP3, WAV etc. Some sites that are worth having a look at are:-

http://www.onhold2go.co.uk

http://www.classiccat.net

https://kamazoy.uk/royalty-free-completely-free-hold-music-mp3-downloads/

Although a lot of the music is free, it is worth checking with the sites first, the last thing the company wants is to be accused of using copyrighted materials without permission.

There are many ways of adding voiceovers to on hold music including using a headset plugged into the audio ports of the PC or using a smart phone to record and download to a PC for mixing.

A freely available open source software called Audicity can be downloaded from:-

http://audacity.sourceforge.net/

One of the staff has used it before and finds it can be very useful for something simple like inserting voice messages into on hold music.

There is a very simple way of creating voice messages by using the actual desk phone to record these messages. As long as mixing background music is not required, voice messages can be recorded the same way as mobile phone or answer phone type prompt messages. For example, recording of voicemail prompt can be done directly from the voicemail menu of the extension.

After studying the manual of the Zycoo U50, the following list of recording is identified and is to be created.

- background on hold music
- welcome message
- "your call is important to us" message
- "office closed message"
- individual voicemail prompts

The U50 supports several music formats:-

- GSM (mobile phone quality)
- WAV (must be 16bit 8KHz Mono)
- uLaw and aLaw

After some research, it is agreed that using a SIP phone to record voice message is more than adequate. So the office is closed message will be recorded just by using Grandstream GXP 1450. Individual extension users will also be using their own SIP phones to record their voicemail message prompt.

A copyright free and usage free classical track is downloaded from the internet and will be used as background on hold music. Insertion of voice welcome message etc. will be done from a PC headset with a good quality microphone.

With the task list completed and a draft of what needs to be done, Mary is ready to put the trial into action.

THE ZYCOO U50

As this is only the trial stage, the U50 was ordered without the BRI and GSM modules to minimise cost. Mary recons that testing the call quality over the internet will probably be adequate since performance of the internet is the main uncertainty and it is believed to be the main factor affecting call quality . The testing of call flows, voicemails etc. will be the same whether the BRI and GSM modules are present or not.

DIAGRAM SHOWING HOW TO CHANGE IP ADDRESS OF THE U50

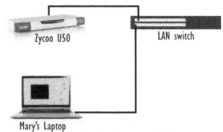

Default ip 192.168.1.100 change to 192.168.6.100 (from Mary's Laptop)

Zycoo U50   LAN switch

Mary's Laptop
Change ip address to 192.168.1.10 to access U50

In order to change the ip address of the U50 to be within the local address, we need Mary's laptop to access the U50 web user interface. Since Mary's lap is configured to obtain ip address automatically, it must be changed to 192.168.1.10 or something so that it is within the same network as the U50.

The U50 is powered up and connected to the local LAN switch via its Ethernet connection. At this stage, it is not part of the LAN and cannot be accessed by any device on the LAN.

Mary now needs to change the ip address of her laptop to be within the network of the U50. The process below is based on Windows 7, the operating system of her laptop. From the desktop, choose the network sharing icon at the bottom right and click "Open Network and Sharing Center" to open the control panel window.

From the "Control Panel Home", choose change adaptor settings.

Control Panel Home

Change adapter settings

Change advanced sharing settings

The next windows displays all available network connections. Choose the correct local network connection by right clicking the Local Area Connection and choose "Properties".

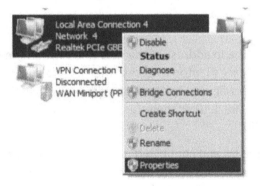

From the "Local Area Connection Properties" window, choose "Internet Protocol Version 4 (TCP/IP) and click "Properties".

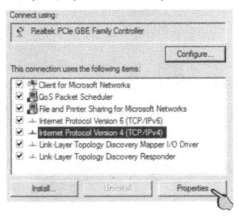

From the "Internet Protocol Version 4 (TCP/IP) Properties" window, change the ip address settings from "Obtain ip address automatically" to "Use the following IP address:" by typing into the correct tabs 192.168.1.10 in the "IP address:" field. There is no need to change the subnet mask. Change the default gateway to 192.168.1.254 (or something other than the ip addresses of the laptop or theU50). Although changing the default gateway makes no difference to whether the laptop can connect to the U50 or not, it stops Windows from throwing up an error warning you that your ip address is in a different network to the default gateway (internet gateway).

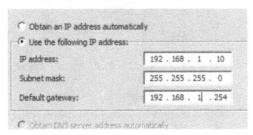

Click OK and Finish to complete the change of settings. As you only want to change this settings to access the U50, there is no need to access the internet at all. Besides, the ip address and default gateway must be changed back to its original settings after the ip address of the U50 is changed anyway. If the laptop ip address setting is not set back to "Obtain ip address automatically", the laptop will effectively be on a different network with no access to any of the network resources at all.

After the change has been made, a browser session is started on Mary's laptop, on this occasion, Firefox is used. Enter the ip address and port of the U50 as show below:-

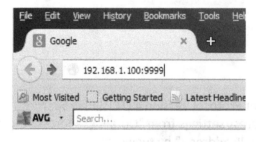

The log in screen of the U50 web interface opens.

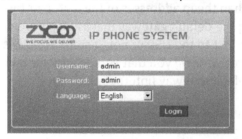

Enter the default username and password, it is usually "admin" for both. However, in case it is not, it is best to check the manual first.

One important tip when configuring the U50 is that when changes are made, you will usually be prompted to activate the changes, unless the

"Activate Changes" button is clicked, the changes may not be properly applied.

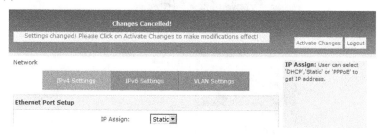

From now on, we will assume that all changes will be properly activated as described above.

Once logged in, click Management on the left hand side and change the admin password from admin to "%_A6m3lTd" as specified in chapter 6.

After changing the admin password, the network settings must be changed to connect the U50 to the network. Next, click the network Settings tab and click network to open the "Network Settings" page.

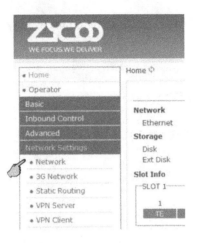

Choose "IPv4 settings" to make changes necessary. Firstly, the "IP Assign:" is set to static. This means the ip address of the U50 will always be the same every time it starts. As specified in Chapter 6, the "IP Address:" is changed to 192.168.6.100, "Subnet Mask" remains the same (255.255.255.0) and "Gateway:" is the router's ip address (192.168.6.254). The setting means the U50 is now at 192.168.6.100 and not 192.168.1.100 and it is using the local router as the default gateway to access the internet. The "Primary DNS" server is the local Microsoft Windows SBS server and the "Alternative DNS" server is the router which acts as the forwarder for the DNS server.

After checking that the addresses are all correct, press "Save" and when prompted to restart, click yes to do so. Once the U50 restarts, the laptop will lose connection to the U50 because the U50 is now part of the local network and the laptop is no longer able to access the U50 as it is on a different network.

Once the restart process begins, the TCP/IP settings of the laptop must be changed back to its original state i.e. using the "Obtain ip address automatically" setting so that it can rejoin the local network again. From now on, the U50 will only be accessible at 192.168.6.100:9999 and by using the new password entered before.

CREATING EXTENSIONS

After changing the network settings and restarting the U50 and the laptop, it is now possible to log in the web user interface of the U50 with the new settings. The next task is to create a few extensions for the trial.

From the main screen, choose "Basic" and then extensions from the left hand menu to open the "Extensions" screen. There are 3 ways of creating extensions. The first is the most basic, manually adding them individually as show by the screens below.

Click "New User" to go to the next screen and manually enter extension details as specified in Chapter 6.

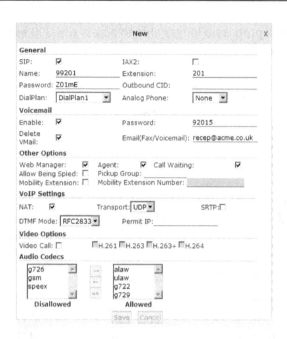

The diagram above shows the configuration of the reception phone which is extension 201. For the trial, the receptionists will have voicemail, but the system will delete any voicemail that's already been sent to the email address of the receptionist (Delete VMail). Since the receptionist will be part of the queuing system in the queue test, "Agent" is ticked to allow her to log in the queue. Unless there are specific reasons to change the default settings, it is best to leave them alone. Click the Save button to create the first user extension.

If there are only a few users in the organisation, this is a very simple and easy way to create extensions. With more than a dozen extensions, Mary decided to use a quicker way of creating extensions for the main office. The U50 allows for the uploading and downloading of extensions to and from it. The main format to create and edit extensions is CSV (comma separated value). This is a pure text format with each field separated by a comma and is supported by many software including

Microsoft Excel. This makes it quite easy for someone like Mary who is very comfortable with Excel to use.

After creating an extension, it is possible to download the extension configuration as a CSV file and modify it or add to it in Microsft Excel and then upload the modified CSV file to complete the creation of the extensions.

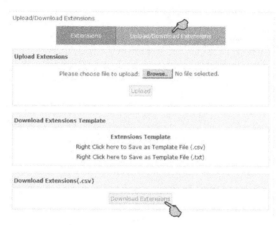

Click on the "Upload/Download Extensions" button to go to the next screen. Click "Download Extensions" to download the CSV file.

After the file is downloaded, it can now be opened in Microsoft Excel as below:-

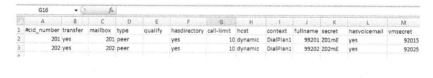

After creating a couple of extensions, the CSV file will look like the above. It is no rocket science to guess what most of the fields mean. By adding all the planned extensions for the main office, Mary is able to create all the extensions within a few minutes.

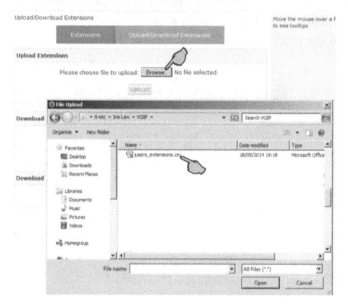

By going to the "Upload/Download Extensions" button again, the new CSV file can be uploaded back to the system and new extensions are now created.

CREATING TRUNKS

The next stage of the trial is to create SIP trunks for the 3 VOIP providers. A SIP Trunk is a connection between two VOIP systems, they can be thought of as telephone lines (just like your normal PSTN lines) except it is possible to make and receive simultaneous calls with one trunk depending on the service with the provider. You need a SIP trunk or line to a VOIP provider in order to make or receive calls through the provider. Although strictly speaking, ACME Ltd. is not using the SIP Trunk service of any of the providers, for configuration purposes, SIP trunks must be created. When configured correctly, these trunks should work just like standard trunks anyway.

From the left hand menu, choose "Basic" and click "Trunks" to go to the next screen. Choose "VoIP Trunks" and click on "New VOIP Trunk".

We will create a trunk for Soho66 first, configuration of the other providers are identical.

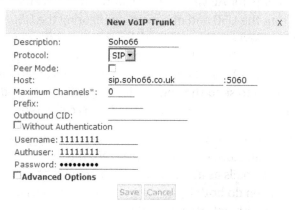

Enter account details as supplied by the provider. It should not be necessary to enter any "Advance Options". Once the correct information is entered for all the providers, the SIP registrations can be checked by going to the Operator menu (Left hand menu, click the "Operator" button. The registration status will display like below:-

VoIP Trunks			
Status	Trunk Name	Type	Username
Registered	Voipfone	SIP	11111111
Registered	Soho66	SIP	11111111
Registered	Draytel	SIP	11111111

By now, the system is configured with the extension details and is registered to all the required SIP servers of the providers.

CONFIGURING VOICEMAIL TO EMAILS

There are two stages to the process of configuring voicemails to be sent as email attachments for ACME Ltd. Configuring the local email server to accept emails from the U50 and of course, configuring the U50 to send emails via the local server. This will work for the main office as the email server is on the local network. For the remote office, the other U50 will have to rely on a smart host (the mail server that sends emails out on behalf of ACME Ltd.) to send the voicemails. This will be covered later when the configuration of the remote office U50 is cofigured.

CONFIGURING THE LOCAL SERVER

Basically, the U50 can store voicemails locally for the extension users or it can send the voicemails as attachments in an email to the specified recipients. It can even do both by keeping the voicemail locally after sending it as an attachment. However, this will mean the extension user must keep deleting voicemails as the system only keeps up to a hundred of them only. But for the trial, it is necessary to keep the voicemails for some users just to confirm the reliability of the process.

ACME Ltd. has a server based on the Microsoft Small Business Server which includes a mail server (Exchange Server) for handling emails. It would make sense to use the local mail server to handle these voicemail emails. As the Exchange Server is not configured to relay emails for the U50, so Mary must configure the Exchange Server to receive voicemail emails from the U50 and send them to the correct recipient's mailbox.

In order to configure the Exchange Server to accept emails from the U50, there must be an "SMTP Receive Connector" available with the correct settings to receive emails from the U50 in order to forward them to the correct recipient.

The server was installed by a local company and has been working reliably from the start. Not wanting to affect the current settings on the Exchange Server, she has decided to create a new receive connector and configure the connector to receive emails from the U50 without authentication to simplify the configuration.

The main reason for creating a new connector is that error in the configuration is unlikely to cause disruption to the company emails and should only affect voicemails from the U50.

The process is done by logging into the server as an administrator and running the Exchange Management Console.

From the left hand menu choose "Server Configuration", click "Hub Transport" to open the right hand pane.

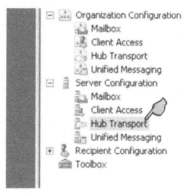

One the right hand pane, from anywhere below the Default receive connector, right click to create a "New Receive Connector".

The new "SMTP Receiver Connector" window will open as below. Enter a name for the connector e.g. Voicemail, choose "Internal" for "Select the intended role for this Receive connector". Since it is only for internal emails (from the U50 to domain users), this setting should be OK. Click "Next".

Remove the "default Remote IP addresses" and add the ip address of the U50 as show below. Click "OK" to continue, click "Next", "New" and then "Finish

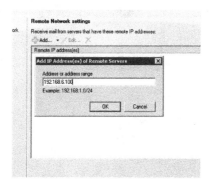

This process has created a new receive connector, but it is not ready to receive and send emails for the U50 yet. By now, there will be two receive connectors for the Exchange Server.

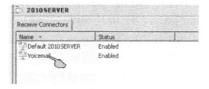

Going back to the "Hub Transport", there is now two receive connectors, the default one and the "Voicemail" which has just been created. Right click on the Voicemail connector and click "Network" to open the "Network" window.

Edit the ip address to something similar to below and click "Apply". "192.168.6.1" is the ip address of the Exchange Server and the ip address of the U50 is "192.168.6.100"

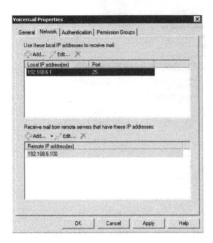

Click the "Permission Groups" tab to open the next window. Mary is going to allow the Exchange Server to receive emails from the U50 without authentication. For testing purposes, it is better for the system to be less complex and hence less to go wrong. Although there is no reason why the receive connector cannot be configured to require authentication by changing the settings in the "Permission Groups" by removing the tick in the "Anonymous" tick box.

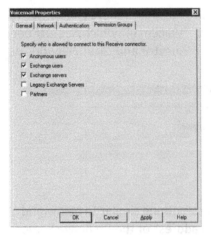

By ticking the "Anonymous users" box, the Exchange Server should accept voicemails from the U50 without authentication and send them to the correct recipient's mailboxes. If this box is not ticked, then the Exchange Server will require correct credentials to receive voicemails from the U50.

The strategy is if this configuration works, it will be left without any more changes. The only potential weakness is that, the Exchange Server is configured to accept emails without authentication. But as it only involves voicemails from the U50 at 192.168.6.100, the security impact is not really going to be serious.

CONFIGURING THE U50 FOR VOICEMAIL AS EMAILS
Log into the U50, choose "Advance" and click "SMTP Settings"

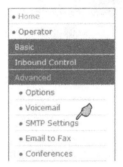

Enter settings as show below and click "Save"

Since the Exchange Server is configured to accept emails from the U50 without authentication, there is no need to enable SMTP Authentication. The U50 should now be able to send voicemails via the Exchange Server.

Finally, the email template should be modified to make it appropriate for ACME Ltd. Due to the explosion of SPAM and Phishing emails that are swarming inboxes, it is extremely important to make it obvious to the staff that the voicemail is from the U50 and not just another bogus email.

To modify the email template, choose "Advance" for the right hand menu, click "Voicemail" to open the next window.

Click the "Email Settings" tab and make required changes as below:-.

GLOBAL SIP CONFIGURATION

The configuration for the U50's SMTP and email settings is now complete. The next stage is to configure the U50 to work correctly over the internet as it needs to be accessible by remote office and remote extensions. The router (firewall) needs to be configured to work with the U50 so it can work efficiently and securely over the internet. Remember, the opening of ports makes the internal network less secure, but in order for the system to work, it is inevitable. So the decision is to open as few ports as possible.

Now there are a couple of factors which may influence the port numbers and the number of ports to be opened. As specified in the security section, the company has chosen port 7655 as a relative safe port to use, so port 7655 of the router must be open at all times.

RTP is used by the system for SIP calls, each call may use up to 4 ports, so adequate number of ports must be allocated. The default settings on the U50 is between 10000 to 20000, so it should be lowered significantly to reflect the actual company needs. It is agreed that 50 ports should be adequate as it will allow for at least a dozen simultaneous calls, three times the estimated average.

Depending on the actual firewall, it may not be necessary to open any ports for RTP at all, so Mary decided to not open those ports initially to see if the system will still work correctly. If this does not work, then the router must be configured with ports opened for RTP.

To access global SIP configuration, go to the left hand menu and click on "Advance", click "Options" to open the next window.

Click "Global SIP Settings" to open the settings window. Modify the following settings:

- Start RTP Port: 10050
- End RTP Port: 10100
- External IP: is the fixed IP assigned by the ISP
- Local Network Address: 192.168.6.0/255.255.255.0

The setting means that the U50 uses 50 ports for RTP from port 10050 to 10100. These ports will need to be open at the firewall if necessary. The external ip address which is the fixed ip assigned by the ISP is 1xx.1xx.6.114 (from now on referred to as external ip)and port 7655 is used. The local network address is the Class C address of "192.168.6.xxx" and the subnet mask is "255.255.255.0".

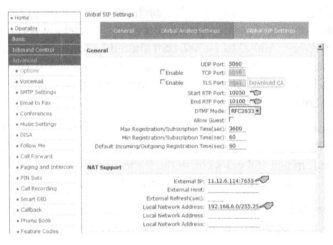

At the bottom, inbound and outbound Sip registrations settings should be set. "Inbound SIP Registrations" as shown in the diagram below is set to allow only 5 attempts for registration of a device and failure to register would mean the device will be blocked for 300 minutes (5 hours) before it is allowed to register again. This is designed to discourage any illegal external attempts to log in to register with the U50.

Global SIP Settings

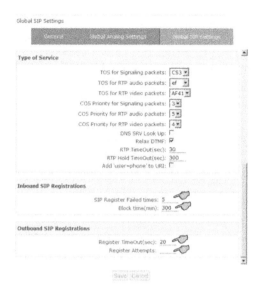

For "Outbound SIP Registrations", "Register TimeOut" is set to 20 seconds, this should be enough to allow for registrations to the providers' SIP servers (trunks). The number of attempts is *left blank to allow for unlimited registration attempts. The reason for unlimited attempts is, in case internet connection is lost for an extended period, the system will continue to attempt to register with the SIP servers until internet connection is restored. Click "Save" when all settings are set.

*This strategy may have an issue which will be revealed later when a deliberate attempt is made to disconnect the internet to simulate the lost of internet connection.

CONFIGURING THE ROUTER/FIREWALL

Like most small organisations, ACME Ltd. uses a single router to access the internet. By using the in-built functions of the router, this also acts as a firewall to protect the local network. The company actually has an extra internet connection to act as back up to the first connection. This is to facilitate remote office and remote users who need access all the time. The second connection is independent and does not have failover capabilities if the first connection fails. Remote users simply log in using a different network connection to access the main office network again.

The U50 will be configured to use the main (faster) internet connection for this trial. The only setting that is required is to use port forwarding to forward UDP packets from port 7655 to port 5060 at 192.168.6.100 of the U50.

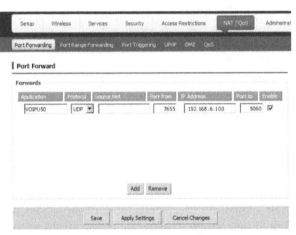

The above diagram shows the port forward settings for the U50 (application name VOIP50).

DIAL PLANS

Put it in very simple terms, a dial plan is a set of rules used by the U50 to control how it will forward calls based on the rules of that plan. In order for any SIP device to make and receive calls, it must use a dial plan, without it, it is useless. Just to add to the confusion, SIP devices like SIP phones have their own dial plans too, so when configuring these devices, consideration must be given to minimise conflicts. For example, some SIP phones are pre-configured with a default dial plan which limits the number of digits dialled to 10, the result is that the SIP phone is not able to make calls if the number being called is over 10 digits long! This is easily addressed by changing the default dial plan or even removing it if necessary.

As the U50 is based on the industry standard Asterisk, all dial plan rules will follow exactly how Asterisk works. A dial plan uses certain characters and numbers to form a pattern, if the pattern is matched by what is dialled, the call will be successful. Some example are shown below:-

- X matches any digit from 0-9
- Z matches any digit from 1-9
- N matches any digit from 2-9
- [1236-8] matches any digit within the brackets (in this example, 1,2,3,6,7,8)
- . wildcard, matches one or more digits (must have at least one digit)
- ! wildcard, matches zero or more characters (can have no digit or any number of digits immediately after)

In addition to the above, dial rules will allow for removing a specified number of digits at the beginning of the dialled numbers or adding a specified number of digits before them.

For example, a user wants to dial a local (Newcastle) number, say the number is "1234567". From a standard telephone, the area code "0191" is not required, so the caller only has to dial "1234567" to make the call. Using IP telephony, the process is just like using a mobile phone, the area code is also needed. So a dial plan for a local number using SIP will require the addition of the area code if the dialled number is a local number.

In order to create a "Dial Plan", it is necessary to create at least one dial rule. By default, the U50 already includes a set of internal dial rules which can be used for the "Dial Plan". We now need to create a dial rule to make external calls through the VOIP providers.

Go to the left hand menu, choose "Basic" then "Outbound Routes", click "DialRules" and then "New DialRule" to open the new dial rule window.

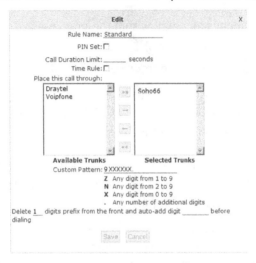

Enter a rule name, let's say "Standard", from the three available trunks under "Place this call through:", choose one e.g. Soho66 by clicking the double right arrows to move it to the "Selected Trunks" on the right hand side.

On the "Custom Pattern:" line, enter something like "9XXXXXX.". At the bottom, enter a "1" in the "Delete" digit prefix. and click "Save".

The settings means that if an extension dials "9" followed by at least 6 digits (between 0 - 9), first remove "1" digit at the beginning (remove "9") and use Soho66 to make this call. The use of dialling "9" to get an external line has been practiced by the company since the beginning, so it was decided to keep the process the same. The use of the local area code must also be used for the trial. When the system is implemented, the dial rules will need to be much more complex to suit the call requirements. So for now, in order to dial the local number of "1234567", the extension will dial "901911234567".

For the trial, all Mary needs to do is to create a simple rule to allow one VOIP provider to be tested at a time. Each provider will be used in turn for a couple of days to evaluate their call quality. So the process of selecting a different trunk for testing every couple of days has to be repeated.

The create a new "Dial Plan" go to left menu again. Choose "Basic", "Outbound Routes", click "DialPlan" and "New DialPlan".

Tick the external dial rule "Standard" and all the internal rules that are relevant for the trial as show below. Click "Save" to complete.

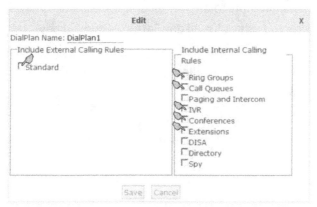

"DialPlan 1" is now created and available for use in the trial. The dial plan will allow all extensions registered with the U50 to receive and make internal and external calls.

TIME BASED RULES

At this stage, it is best to assess what is needed to make a time based rule useful. A time based rule allows the telephone system to operate according to a set of pre-defined operations. To make it appropriate for ACME Ltd., any time based rules must be personalised for the company including any voice messages or instructions.

What the company wants is to be able to give callers a more professional response after working hours. The current process of the standard answer phone response can be changed to allowing the caller to actively choose to leave a message or hang up. This will minimise the blank voice messages when the caller hangs up without leaving a message with the current system. In addition, it saves the receptionists from having to manually switch the phone system to answer phone on and off every working day.

How the time rules should work can be shown below:-

- automatically start at 9.00am (Monday to Friday) and forward all calls to the receptionist
- automatically start to answer incoming calls after 5.00pm (Monday to Friday plus all day Saturday and Sunday).
- on receiving a call, plays a welcome message (IVR Prompt)
- at the end of message, allow callers to press "0" to leave a voicemail

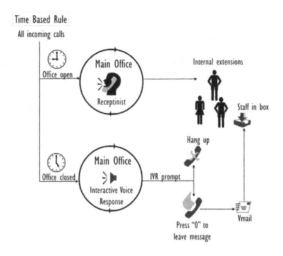

OPENING HOURS

What are the requirements:-

- predefined opening and closing hours (Time Based Rule)
- IVR (Interactive Voice Response or Auto Attendant)
- IVR prompt (Welcome Message)
- caller option to leave a message
- predefined extension for callers to leave voicemails

Since the office is not open 24 hours a day and seven days a week, it is therefore necessary to split the day into opening and closed hours. The main office is open between 9.00am and 5.00pm Monday to Friday. After 5.00pm everyday and before 9.00am the next morning, the office will close and there will be no one assigned to answer calls. The same will go for all day Saturdays and Sundays.

A time based rule can be created to handle incoming calls during opening hours and closing hours as specified in the plan. The plan calls for routing incoming calls to reception in two ways - "Ring Group" and

"Queue". Since the opening and closing hours are identical, only one rule is needed.

CREATE A NEW "TIME BASED RULE"
Go to left hand menu and choose "Inbound Control", "Time Based Rules" and click "New Time Rule" to open new time rule window.

Enter settings as below:-

A new rule called "Standard" has been created, the rule specifies that during opening hours, all calls will be answered by extension 201, if not, they will go to an IVR called "closed time". This IVR is one of the default IVRs available and needs to be changed to suit the requirements of ACME Ltd. If it is not there, then "closed time" will not be on the list of "if time does not match", then a new IVR called "closed time" should be created.

To modify the current "closed time" IVR, go to left menu, choose "Inbound Control", "IVR" to open the "List of IVRs". Click "Edit" to open the next window.

If "closed time" is not available, click "New IVR" to open the next window and create it. Since the time rule "Standard" above specified that an IVR called "closed time" is to be used, an IVR called "closed time" must be on the list of "if time does not match".

Edit the settings to something similar to below. Since it is necessary to create the voice "Welcome Message" or IVR prompt, choose "Custom Prompt" and select an available IVR prompt since the default IVR Prompts are not designed for ACME Ltd.

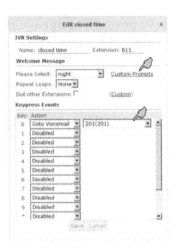

The IVR above specifies that an IVR prompt (Welcome Message) will play, the caller will be prompted to either call back or leave a voicemail (for extension 201).

It is now necessary to modify the default "night" IVR prompt (Welcome Message) to make it appropriate for the company. The message should be something like thanking the caller for calling, inform the caller that the office is shut and then the caller will be asked to either call back or press "0" to leave a voicemail. If the "night" IVR Prompt is not available, simply create one using the steps shown below.

RE-RECORD OR CREATE A NEW AN IVR PROMPT (WELCOME MESSAGE),

Go to left hand menu, choose "Basic", "Inbound Control", "IVR Prompts"
and choose the prompt to be changed, click "Record Again" to continue.
A new window will open as below.

Click "OK" to confirm overwriting the current file to go to the next
screen. Choose the extension to record the sound, on this occasion,
extension 201 is chosen as it seems to have the best call quality.

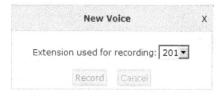

Click "Record", the extension will ring with a prompt to start recording.
After recording, it is possible to listen to the recording again by pressing
"Play".

When prompted, choose an extension to play the recorded message.
The extension will then ring and the recorded message will play. The IVR
prompt is now ready to be used.

To create a new IVR Prompt, "New Voice" and follow the exact process as replacing an IVR Prompt.

CALL QUEUE
Routing incoming calls
The next stage is to route all incoming calls to the correct extension/s for the trial. Remember there are 2 processes to be tested, "Ring Group" and "Call Queues".

CREATING "RING GROUP"
"Ring Group" requires all incoming calls to be routed to the receptionist first and then to the "Secretaries Ring Group" if the receptionist is not available. Go to left hand menu, choose "Inbound Control" and "New Ring Group".

The first "Ring Group" to be created is "Receptionist". From the "New Ring Group" window , choose extension 201 from the "Available Channels" on the right hand side by clicking 201(SIP) and the left arrow to move it to the "Ring Group Members" on the left hand side. Change the timing to something like 30 seconds for the "Ring (each/all) for lasting time(sec):" and leave the "If not answered" setting to just the default. This needs to be changed to the "Secretaries Ring Group" later in order for unanswered calls from "Reception" to be forwarded to the "Secretaries Ring Group" later.

Click "Save" to save the "Reception Ring Group" settings. Looking at the diagram below, the "Reception" ring group has another extension which is "640". This means that extension 640 can be dialled internally to reach extension 201, currently the only extension in the "Reception" ring group.

Create the "Secretaries Ring Group" by following the same procedure as above. This time, the "If not answered" section should be configured to "Goto Ring Group" and the "Ring Group" chosen should be "Reception" which has just been created.

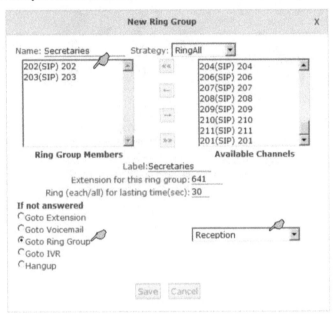

After creating the "Secretaries Ring Group", go back to change the settings of the "Reception Ring Group" to forward unanswered calls in the "If not answered" section to "Secretaries Ring Group" and click "Save".

Both the "Secretaries Ring Group" and the "Reception Ring Group" have been successfully created now.

"RING GROUP" DEFAULT ROUTE FOR INCOMING CALLS
The next stage is to create a default route for all incoming calls. Go to left hand menu and choose "Inbound Control", "Inbound Routes" and

click "General". As extension 201 is to be used as "Reception", all incoming calls will be answered by extension 201 by default.

The U50 is now configured to forward all incoming calls to extension 201 (Reception), if the call is not answered within 30 seconds, it will be forwarded to extension 202 and 203 simultaneously (Secretaries). If the call is still not answered after 30 seconds, it will go back to extension 201 again.

"CALL QUEUE"

For an alternative call flow, call queuing will be configured. Looking at the call flow using "Ring Groups", it is noted that a caller will hear only ringing until someone answers the call. This is really no different to the conventional system currently being used. The trial using "Ring Groups" is to be only used as a template for reference only.

The company wants to improve caller experience by getting all incoming calls to be answered immediately by a "Call Queue". The caller will then be held in a queue until the receptionist answers the call. By having a voice message and background music soon after a caller's call is connected, the caller's experience will be much improved. In addition, the management is considering some sort of marketing message to be included too.

CREATING THE WELCOME MESSAGE WITH BACKGROUND MUSIC

Before creating a call queue, voice message with background "on hold" music needs to be generated. As specified in the plan, Mary downloaded several suitable tracks from one of the websites offering "free to use" on hold music. At the same time several voice messages are recorded on one of the company laptops using a good quality PC microphone.

Using open source (Audacity) software to create the company's own on hold music

The music chosen to be used as background music is loaded into Audicity by opening it as shown below

It is best to always work on the highest possible quality, so the sampling rates etc. is left at default for the time being. Since the U50 and telephones work in mono, the music needs to be converted to mono.

Remove one of the music tracks by clicking the "x" as show below to simplify the screen. Make sure the quality of the remaining track is good enough.

The volume level of the music can be adjusted by using the envelope tool. By click on the appropriate position to add a point, the volume of the music can be adjusted at the specified point. The diagram below shows an increase in volume towards 35 seconds.

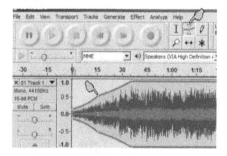

By adjusting the volume of the background music at the right locations, voice messages can be placed and mixed with the background music.

Go to "File" and click "Import" to choose the voice message previously recorded.

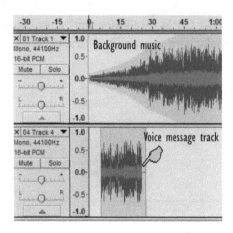

Use the "Selection tool" to highlight the "Voice message track" above to select the voice that is required. Then click "Copy" and paste the selected sound track into the

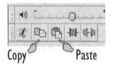

Copy   Paste

relevant location of the background music track.

The background music track should look something like the following.

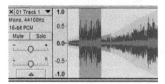

Make sure the "Voice message" sound track is removed by clicking the "x", leaving only the mixed voice and music sound track. Listen to the track and make sure the quality of the voice message over the background music is good enough. It is now time to save the music in a format that the U50 can use. It does not matter what original format the tracks are in, they must be "16bit 8KHz wave" with a suffix of .wav for the U50.

Choose "Edit" from the top and click on "Preference..." to open the "Preference" settings window.

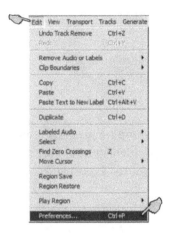

Set "Quality" to 8KHz, 16-bit as shown below.

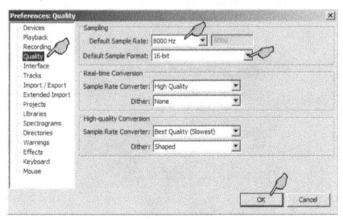

At the bottom left of the screen, set project rate to 8KHz as below.

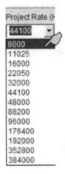

Once the format is set, the sound track needs to be exported as one file. By using the "Selection Tool", highlight the part of the track to be exported. Go to "File" and choose "Export selection". If the whole track is needed, just choose "Export".

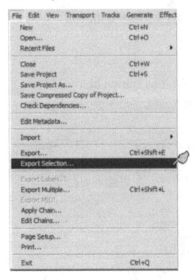

Make sure the file is exported as 16 bit .wav format.

Edit the "Metadata" if desired and click "OK" to save the file.

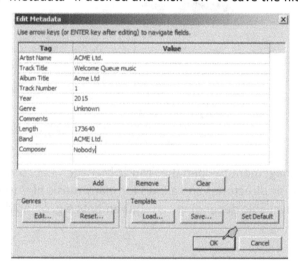

Just to confirm that the file is saved correctly, open the file (ACME.wav) again and check to see if it is 16 bit 8KHz Mono wave format. The format should display the following format on the left hand side of the track.

Once the quality and format of the background music and message is approved, it needs to be uploaded to the U50. Go to the left hand menu, choose "Advanced" and "Music Settings".

Click Music Management to open the "Music Management" screen. The U50 has ten music directories and allows for many music files to be stored and be available depending on requirements e.g. on hold music etc.

To eliminate any confusion, Mary decides to choose an empty directory and put the "Queue Music" there. A safe bet is to use something like "Music 9". To confirm that it is empty, click "Load" to see if any music file loads. Once it is confirmed that the directory is empty, select "Music 9" in the "Select Music Directory" tab and click browse to choose the file to upload.

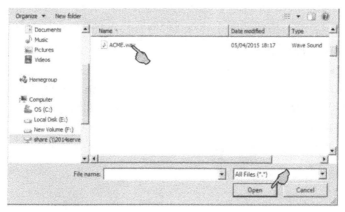

Once the file is loaded successfully to the U50, it is available to be used as the "Queue Music". Click "Music Settings" to go to the "Music Settings" page. In the "Music On Queue Reference" section, choose

"Music 9" and click "Save". This means that the queue music with inserted welcome greetings called "ACME.wav" will be played as soon as the "Call Queue" answers incoming calls.

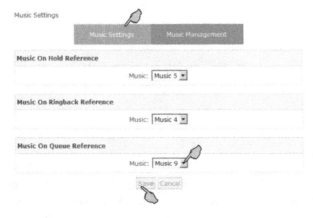

The "Music Settings" page can also be used to choose on hold music. The same process of using Audacity can be used to generate on hold music and then set in this page. Just choose whichever music directory the on hold music is uploaded to e..g. "Music 5" above.

CONFIGURING THE "CALL QUEUE"

The U50 by default already has three "Call Queues" available for use. In order to use "Call Queue", it is necessary to modify one of them and configure it to suit the need of ACME Ltd. Go to the left hand menu, choose "Inbound Control" and click "Call Queue".

Click "Call Queue 1" to open the configuration page for "Queue Number 630". The management has decided that the "Call Queue" last for 4 minutes with the queue music and voice message playing in the background while the caller is placed on hold. They also do not think there is a need for "Caller Position Announcement" or other "Periodic Announcement" at this stage. The settings should be something like the following diagram:-

The diagram above shows there is only one agent (extension 201) for this queue. However, if necessary, extension 202 and 203 can become agents too. Anyone can be an agent to the "Call Queue" as long as the "Agent" check box is ticked in the extension settings page for that particular extension. The "Call Queue" is ready to go into operation for the second stage of the trial now.

SUMMARY OF ALL THE PREPARATION WORK FOR THE TRIAL
The U50 is now all set up and is configured to do the following:-

- accessing the internet
- accept registrations from internal and external SIP devices
- able to use the Exchange Server to send voicemails as emails

- established SIP trunks to three VOIP providers to allow for outgoing and incoming calls
- created a simple dial plan with an outgoing dial rule as well as internal ones
- configured firewall to open port 7655 and forward UDP packets to the U50
- operate in a reasonably secure state with relevant defaults changed

All that is left now is to configure the SIP devices (phones) to register with the U50 before testing call quality. It is relatively simple to connect/register a SIP Phone to the U50 on the LAN as it does not require traversing firewalls etc. Configuration of SIP Phones for remote workers may be more complex as registration to the U50 and communications using various ports has to go through the router/firewall.

LAN based SIP Phones

Configuring the Grandstream GXP 2160 (for reception)

As the easiest way to configure the SIP Phone is to use the web user interface, the first task is to actually locate the ip address SIP Phone. There are several ways to identify it, the easiest is via its keyboard. Press the big round button to bring up menu on the LCD screen.

Go to "Status" and press "Network status" to display ip address. Then from a browser on a local PC, type in the ip address to bring up the web user interface log in screen.

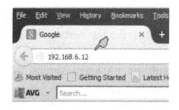

Log in screen opens

Enter the default username (usually "admin") and password (usually "admin") usually. Once logged in, go to "Maintenance" and click on "Web Access" change the "admin" password to what is specified in the security section of the plan i.e. "aCmEltd". Click "Save" to complete the change.

Optionally, the basic network settings can be set to use a fixed ip address for easier management. Go to "Network" and click "Basic Settings" to open the following screen. Tick "Statically configured as" and enter the ip address, subnet mask etc. similar to below:-

The main reason for using fixed ip addresses is that the devices can be managed by using their web user interface without having to go to the device to find out its ip address. This means that Mary can manage all the SIP Phones on the LAN from her desk.

Mary has also decided to leave all settings to default unless there is a requirement to change it. The next step is to activate the first account to register to the U50.

Go to "Account" and click "General Settings", enter details as below or something similar. Click the "Yes" radio button and then "Save and Apply".

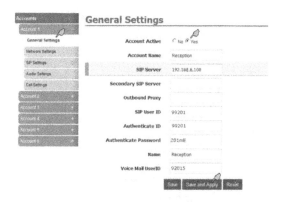

In a few moments, the GXP 2160 would be registered with the U50 and will be ready to make and receive calls. To confirm that it is registered, log into the U50 by using the web user interface. On the left hand menu, choose "Report" and click "Register Status". Click "SIP User Status" to display the following screen. Extension 201 is registered and its "Status" is show as "OK".

To confirm that the system is ready to make and receive external calls, click on "SIP Trunk Status".

The trunk status is shown to be registered and the U50 is now ready to allow extension 201 to make and receive calls, internally as well as externally.

A few outgoing calls and incoming calls confirms that the system is working correctly and the call quality is probably as good as their current system. It is very difficult to tell the difference if any, as the GXP 2160 sounds slightly different to their current telephones, the staff who tried it cannot say whether it is better or worse.

Configuring other SIP Phones

CONFIGURING YEALINK T20
As with the GXP 2160, identify the ip address by press the round "OK" button.

Using a browser, type in the ip address to access the web user interface to the log in screen.

The default username and password is usually just "admin", check the documentation first, just in case it is different. Enter the username and password and click confirm to log in.

Once logged in, click on "Security" and "Password" to change to the default password.

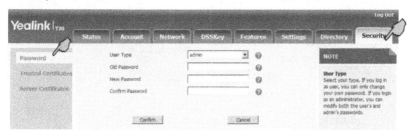

Click "Confirm to finish. The next stage is to configure the T20 to register with the U50. Go to "Account" and enter necessary details.

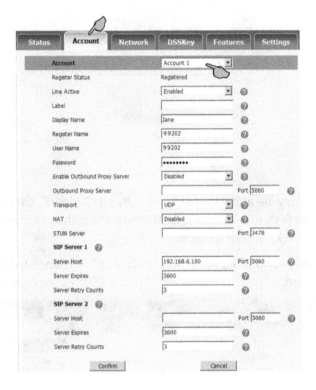

Press "Confirm" to complete.

The "Account Status" should now show that "Account1" is now registered with the U50. Confirmation that both the extensions are working correctly and check quality by calling each other. By default the "#" key is used to "send" the call, the same as pressing the dial key on mobiles. This tells the SIP Phone to call immediately and not wait a few seconds to confirm the number dialled is complete e.g. 201# to call extension 201.

CONFIGURING THE POLYCOM SOUNDPOINT IP 331

The process of configuring the Polycom is similar to the other SIP Phones, to get the phone's IP address, it is necessary to do it on phone itself, do the following:

- press the "Menu" key, and then
- choose "Status",
- choose "Platform"
- choose "Phone"
- Scroll down to see the IP address

To change the default password to the password set by the security policy in the plan, it has to be done on the phone itself, the procedures are as follows:-

- press "Menu" button
- choose option 3 - "Settings"
- then choose option 2 - "Advanced"
- enter the default admin password - usually "456"
- choose option 1 - "Admin Settings"
- then option 6 - "Change Adm P/W"
- enter the default password , set new password and confirm new password to complete

The Polycom is now ready to be configured. Open a browser and enter the ip address of the phone in the address bar.

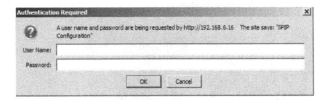

The default username is usually "Polycom" and enter new the password entered before and click "OK" to log in.

After logging in, go to "SIP", "Local Settings" and remove everything in the digitmap section.

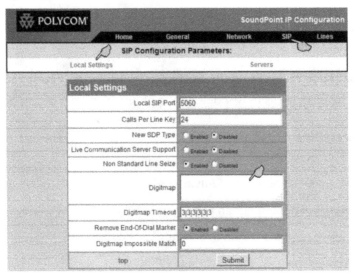

Click "Submit", next click "Servers", choose "Server1" and enter settings as below:-

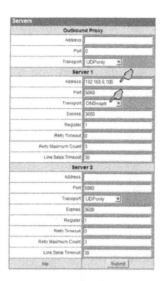

Click "Submit " when completed.

Go to "Lines", choose "Line 1" and enter settings as below:-

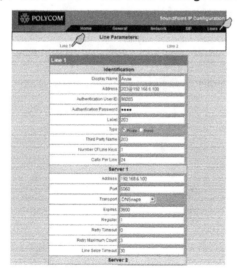

Once all settings are completed, press "Confirm" to finish. The Polycom is now ready to make and receive calls.

CONFIGURING THE GRANDSTREAM GXP 1450

The configuration of the Grandstream GXP 1450 is almost identical to that of the GXP 2160.

- indentify the ip address by pressing "OK" button on the phone
- use browser to log in to the web user interface
- change password
- change network settings from DHCP to fixed ip if desired
- enter settings for the extension

CONFIGURING MOBILE SOFTPHONE APP

For the mobile extensions, the "Grandstream Wave App" needs to be configured. The app is freely downloadable from the Google App Store.

Using an smart phone (Android OS), download the app from the App Store. Once the download is completed, run the app.

Go to settings at the bottom of the screen

Tab the "Account Settings"

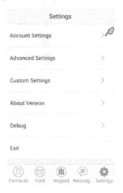

Tab "Add New Account" to create one, enter settings that are specified in the plan as below:-

Note that the "SIP Server" setting is the external ip address of the router at the main office using port 7655. Once all account settings are entered, activate the account. The mobile phone app will register with the U50 and the mobile phone becomes extension 261 as specified in the plan.

CONFIGURE REMOTE SIP PHONE

For the trial, one of the GXP 1450 is located at the home of one of the remote workers. Since the phone is outside the local network, the settings has to be slightly different.

Log into the phone by using its web user interface, go to "Accounts", click "Account 1" to edit settings below:-

Note the external ip address is the external ip address of the router at the main office. Port used is 7655, so the setting for the "SIP Server" is identical to that of the mobile app. According to the plan specified, the setting should look something like the diagram above.

An extra step is used here just in case there may be issues with the local firewall/router at the remote user's home. For remote extensions, a STUN server is configured in the settings of the SIP Phone.

STUN server - Session Traversal of User Datagram Protocol (UDP) through Network Address Translators (NAT) server allows NAT clients (i.e. IP Phones behind a firewall) to setup phone calls to a VoIP provider hosted outside of their local network.

To put it in very simple terms, a Stun server is a helper for two devices (SIP Phones) behind NAT firewalls to communicate correctly with each other .

In order to use a STUN server, the phone needs to be configured to use one. There are many public STUN servers available and Mary choice was stun.sipgate.net. To add a STUN server, go to "Settings" and click "General Settings"

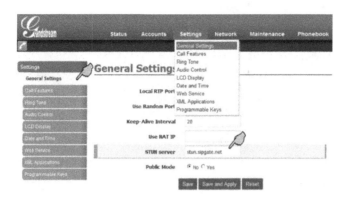

Enter "stun.sipgate.net" in the "STUN server" box and click "Save and Apply". The above step may not be necessary, it is taken just in case it helps. It should not cause the SIP Phones to not work if it is not needed.

Once all the SIP devices are set up and connected, log into the U50 as normal, click "Operator" on the left hand menu to display the status of all the available extensions.

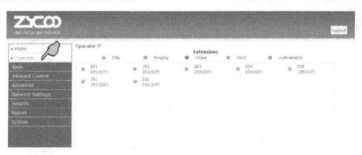

The above diagram displays an operator's view of the system and shows all the available extensions that are registered to it. The next thing to do is to invoke the "Time Based Rules" for opening and closing hours. Referring to the "Time Based Rules" screen, "Enable Office Closed Time" can be set by dialling "*81" on the reception phone, so *81" is dialled to enable this rule.

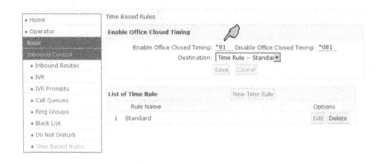

The reception SIP Phone extension 201 should now be configured to monitor the other extensions by using the "BLF" buttons.

Log into the web user interface of extension 201 by using its ip address. Go to "Settings" and choose "Programmable Keys"

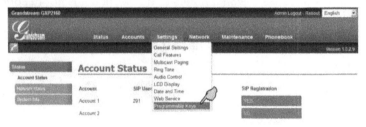

In the "Multi-Purpose Keys" section, input the settings as the diagram below:-

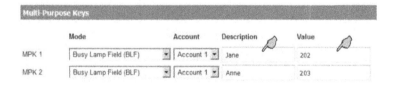

The keys are programmable and can have several "Modes" such as "Speed Dial" or "Voicemail" etc. Enter "Description" to describe what the button shows and the "Value" where value is the extension number. The diagram above shows that the BLF light is for monitoring Jane's extension which is extension 202.

The GXP 2160 can have up six accounts, since "Account 1" is configured to register with the U50, this account must be used.

Once the programmable keys are set, the BLF light for an individual extension will light up when it is registered to the U50 as shown below:-

The system is now fully ready for the trial. As the remote office staff and remote worker regularly calls the main office, they will be the main candidates to participate in the trial. In addition, friends and some regular clients have also been asked to make calls to the VOIP numbers to add extra participants to the trial.

The first stage of the trial is for all incoming calls to go to the "Reception Ring Group", if it is not answered within the number of seconds specified in the extension settings, the calls will be forwarded to the "Secretaries Ring Group". Since the settings have already been done previously, there is no need to make any changes to the "Inbound Route" settings.

Calls are made from the remote office and all other participants over the next two weeks using all three different VOIP providers. This is achieved by changing the trunk settings for the different providers every three days during and out of office hours.

Call conferencing is tested several times by the following method:-

- logging into the default conference room extension 900 by dialling 900#
- entering the "Administrator Password" of "2345"

- invite the other people into the conference by dialling "0" + user's number followed by "**"

The default conference settings worked correctly and the call quality seemed good. However, the test revealed an issue which should be addressed. The main concern is the default administrator's password of "2345" which is very similar to the guest password of "1234".

There is also concerns of security over using a default password. The confusion of the guest password and the administrator's password manifested when Mary logged into the default conference using "1234", assuming that she was using the administrator's password. It took many failed attempts to invite people for conferencing before it was realised that she was using the incorrect password. Guests do not have the permission to invite other people to join a conference, hence the failures. It is therefore decided to change the default password to something easy to remember but not simple.

CALL CONFERENCEING

Configure conferencing by going to the left hand menu and choosing "Advance"

There must be a "Conference DialPlan" which allows dialling external numbers, to allow the administrator to invite people outside the office to join a conference. "DialPlan 1" is chosen as this is currently the default and it allows for external calls through the VOIP providers.

After the test has been completed, the results are shown below:-

- quality of calls over the internet (good with all three providers)
- quality of internal calls (good)
- voice to emails operation (works reliably and sound quality good)
- voice messages accessed from the extensions (good)
- call quality of mobile extensions (poor on the SIP Phone extension side)
- call quality of remote extensions (good)
- use of music on hold (works reliably)
- use of ring groups   (works reliably)
- use of BLF lights to monitor extension status (issues)
- use of time based rules (works reliably)
- use of call conferencing (works correctly as expected)

Voicemails can be accessed from an extension by dialling *60 and entering the extension number and voicemail password from the extension (do not press "#" after extension number and password).

The second stage of the trial is utilising "Call Queue". In order to invoke the queue, go to the left hand menu, choose "Inbound Routes", "General" and choose "Goto Queue" and use 630 (default) as the extension.

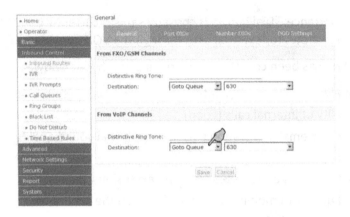

As the quality of calls is no longer part of the trial, only trunk from VOIP provider Soho66 is used for this test. The reason for using Soho66 is that it offered the best package for the company. One week is allocated for this test.

Apart from the fact that the reception is under pressure to transfer all calls as quickly as possible, the test confirms that all functions of the system works correctly as expected, however there are several serious issues that need to be addressed.

The issues are:-

- call quality issue with using "Grandstream Wave"
- when internet connection is removed to simulate an internet failure, all extensions lost registrations with the U50 after a minute or so
- when one of the extensions was disconnected accidentally, the reception phone (Grandstream GXP 2160) went on and off line at random intervals.

Although the call quality issue with the mobile app is not critical, the other issues are and they must be addressed fully otherwise the project must be cancelled.

CALL QUALITY OF MOBILE APP

To address the call quality with the mobile app, Mary decides to try a paid for app by Counterpath called Bria Android Edition for under £6. The process of configuration is the same as configuring the Grandstream Wave. The default call quality is good enough without needing to make any adjustments to the settings. The company therefore decided to use this app for all mobile users.

LOSING ALL EXTENSIONS AFTER LOSING INTERNET CONNECTION

A quick search on the internet shows that this is a bug on the Asterisk system. As the U50 is based on Asterisk, it suffers the same problem. According to the Asterisk.org website - " Asterisk stops responding to SIP devices if it loses Internet Access (DNS)". Apparently, it has existed for a while and has not been addressed yet. The problem appears to be if the internet connection is down, the U50 cannot resolve the VOIP trunk's domain name of sip.soho66.co.uk to its ip address of "84.45.53.115"

The ironic situation here is that, the U50 does not actually need internet access to continue operating, it just needs the DNS for its VOIP trunk resolved. Basically, the U50 only needs to know where sip.soho66.co.uk is, but it does not need to go there. So whilst it is not possible to connect remote extensions and VOIP trunks with internet access, the main office telephone system (U50 and extensions) can still function without the internet.

This is extremely important for the final operational VOIP system as it needs to run reliably all the time. Since it can make use of ISDN and mobile SIMs, it will not become inoperable without internet an connection.

There are several potential solution to solve this issue:-

- modify local DNS server to allow U50 to resolve sip.soho66.co.uk
- have a second internet connection using a different service provider so if one connection goes down, the second can be used
- use ip address for VOIP trunk instead of sip.soho66.co.uk

- edit the host file of the U50 to resolve the SIP trunk sip.soho66.co.uk
- change the external timing for registration with the VOIP trunk

Since ACME Ltd. has a Microsoft Windows SBS server which includes DNS service, it should be possible to just configure the server so that it can resolve DNS for the U50. However, different consideration has to be given to the remote office as it does not have the benefit of a local DNS server, so it has to be configured differently.

CONFIGURE DNS ON THE WINDOWS SBS SERVER

For the main office, a new "Forward Lookup Zone" is required to resolve the ip address of the VOIP trunk sip.soho66.co.uk. To do so log into the server and run the DNS manager as below:-

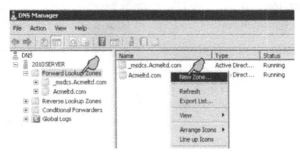

On the right hand pane, choose "Forward Lookup Zones" and on the right hand pane, right click to create a "New Zone".

Choose "Primary Zone" as the Zone Type.

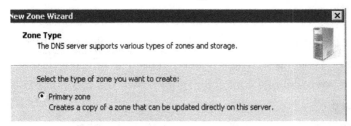

Click "Next", leave default value of "To all DNS servers running on domain controllers in this domain .

Click "Next" to and enter "Zone name:" "sip.soho66.co.uk" as below:-

Click "Next"to go to "Dynamic Update" section and choose "Do not allow dynamic updates"

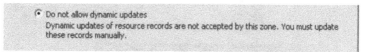

Click "Next" and then "Finish".

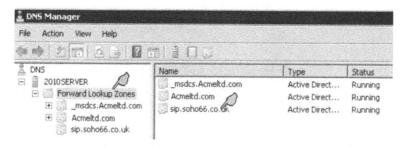

Go back to "Forward Lookup Zones" and open sip.soho66.co.uk on the right hand pane. Right click to choose "New Host (A or AAAA)...." to add a new host record.

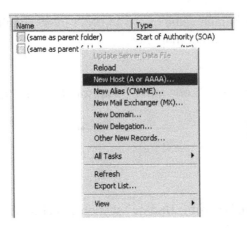

Enter the ip address of "sip.soho66.co.uk" as below:-

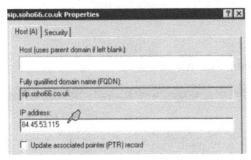

Click "OK" to finish. The DNS server will now be able to resolve "sip.soho66.co.uk" to its ip address even if there is no internet connection. As this is the "Primary DNS server" for the U50, it should allow the U50 to continue working even without an internet connection.

The second solution to solve the internet failure issue for the U50 is the easiest and possibly the best. The company has always had two internet connections for both sites. The idea is to allow remote office and users to be able to connect to a back up internet connection should the main connection fails.

The solution is to use the second internet connection's router to act as one of the DNS server. This means that instead of having to depend on having a local DNS server like the main office server, both offices can make use of both available routers as their DNS servers.

With this solution, only the U50's network settings need to be configured. The process is the same as the original process of configuring the "Network" settings. This time the second router's ip address (192.168.6.250) is used as the "Primary DNS" as below:-

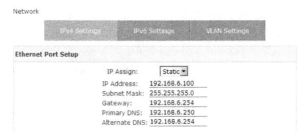

The third potential solution is to use the ip address instead of the domain name (sip.soho66.co.uk). Replace the "Host" with the ip address of "84.45.53.115" as shown below:-

Unfortunately, not all SIP servers accept registrations using ip addresses and the Soho66 sip server is one of them, so on this occasion, this method does not work.

The fourth potential solution is to edit the hosts file of the U50 itself, so instead of trying to resolve the ip address of the VOIP trunk by using a DNS server, it is resolved locally without having to access the internet.

The hosts file of the U50 can be edited by using SSH. Secure Shell (SSH), also known as Secure Socket Shell. There are several open source Windows clients which are freely downloadable. Mary's choice is WinSCP from winscp.net which is downloaded at http://winscp.net/eng/docs/free_ssh_client_for_windows.

In order to access the files in the U50, the username and password is required. By default, the username is "root" and the password is the last eight digits (without the colons) of the MAC address of the U50. This can be located at the home page of the user interface under "System Info".

The password for this particular U50 is therefore "2E2E0DAA". After noting down the password, go to the "Security", "Services" and "Service Settings" to enable SSH.

For security reason, it may be a good idea to disable SSH after completing the next stage. Note that port 22 is used, so make sure that the SSH client also uses port 22 to connect to the U50.

After downloading and installing "Winscp" configure a new site and input details as below:-

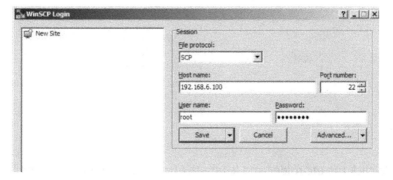

Click "Save" and give the site a name to finish. Tick the boxes to save the password and create a desktop icon.

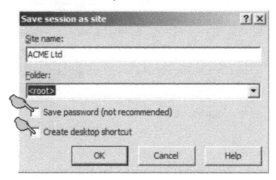

They can be deleted after the session is finished. This makes it simpler as it is likely that this session is the only one required.

Double click the desktop icon created to log in to the U50, locate the hosts file in the etc folder, just like a Windows system except the U50 etc folder is located in the top level /< root>.

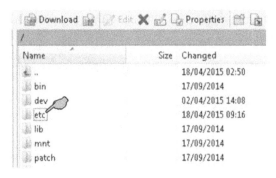

Double click the etc folder and locate the hosts file. Right click on the hosts file and choose "Edit" to open the file for editing.

Add the ip address and domain name of the VOIP provider to the hosts file as below:-

Save the file to finish. Now the U50 should be able to resolve sip.soho66.co.uk to its ip address without requiring a DNS server.

The final potential solution to the internet failure issue affecting the U50 is to change the external number of attempts for "Outbound Sip Registrations" as pointed out earlier in the "Global Sip Settings" section. By reducing the number of attempts to register with the external VOIP provider to something like three attempts, the U50 should stop registration attempts after 60 seconds or so and start to work again.

However, this solution is a non starter as someone has to manually re-register with the VOIP provider again after internet connection is restored. In addition, if internet connection is lost after opening hours or even for just a few minutes, VOIP registration to the VOIP provider will be lost. This may create a confusing situation where internet is working but the U50 is not registered with the VOIP provider.

The choice by the management to address the internet connection failure is to utilise both the internet connections for the offices. This solution requires no manual effort and is reliable, after all, it is unlikely for both internet connections from different providers to fail at the same time.

BLF LAMP CAUSING THE RECEPTION **SIP** PHONE TO LOSE REGISTRATION ISSUE
This can be addressed by using the "BLF patch" supplied by the supplier of the U50. The patch arrived as an attachment from an email. This patch should be applied with the "Web Upgrade". Go to "System" on the U50, choose "System" and "Upgrade"

Locate the file below and click "Upload" to apply the patch.

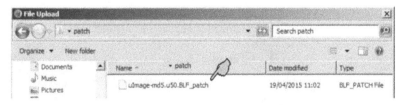

The BLF lights on the Grandstream GXP 2160 is now working properly even if an extension has gone off line.

Final check from the checklist:-

- quality of calls over the internet (good)
- quality of internal calls (good)
- voice to emails operation (works reliably and sound quality good)
- voice messages accessed from the extensions (good)
- call quality of mobile extensions (addressed)
- call quality of remote extensions (good)
- use of music on hold (works reliably)
- use of ring groups/ call queue (works reliably)
- use of BLF lights to monitor extension status (solved)
- use of time based rules (works reliably)
- use of call conferencing (works correctly as expected)

After checking to make sure that all the devices are working and all the settings are correct, the trial is now complete and the company is ready to implement the VOIP system at their new premises.

CHAPTER 8

ROLL OUT

On completing the trial to evaluate the quality of calls and the operating process, the management is satisfied with everything and is confident of a successful implementation. The next stage is to order all equipment and install them at the new main office and the remote office. During the trial, there appears to be no significant difference between the call quality of the different brands SIP Phones, as a result, the lowest cost SIP Phone (GXP 1450) is chosen as the standard desk phone for the company.

Mary ordered all the equipment that are necessary for the two offices and the remote workers.

List of equipment and apps to purchase are:-

- 2 X ZYCOO CooVox U50 PBX
- 2X 4 BRI ISDN modules
- 2 X 2GSM modules
- 2 X Grandstream GXP 2160
- 18 X Grandstream GXP 1450
- 3 X UPS APC BE550G-UK
- 2 X 24 port switches
- 4 X Bria for Android Edition
- 20 X "Flat" CAT5 cables

Any spares e.g. an extra U50 and UPS can be purchased at a later stage , after the implementation.

Since Mary is not sure which mobile network operator offers the best quality, she has decided to initially test the call quality of the providers first by purchasing prepaid SIMs from two providers - three and EE. The reason for choosing these two providers is that their local masts are all within two or three hundred metres of the offices.

Implementing the U50
Since the U50 at the main office has already been configured for some of the functions, Mary decides to implement the main office U50 first. This unit requires two modules to operate as planned, the GSM module (mobile calls) and the BRI module (ISDN). Both these modules needs to slot into the available slots on the back of the U50. Note that the BRI module must be installed into Slot 1. So the GSM module will be installed in slot2. Remember to switch the U50 off and unplug it first.

The GSM module
In order for the GSM module to make mobile calls, a valid SIM with available call credits must be installed onto the module itself. There are two available slots for SIMs so two simultaneous calls can be made by the system. The process of installing the SIMs is almost identical to inserting a SIM into a mobile phone. The SIMs have to be activated first, it is best for both the SIMs to be activated and set up correctly on a mobile phone before installing them. One of the staff has an unlocked mobile, so both the SIMs can be set up with the same phone.

Once both the SIMs are properly installed, the module can then be inserted into slot 2 at the back of the U50. Remove the two red plastic covers and connect the supplied aerials to the aerial connections, place the aerials on top of the U50 or anywhere appropriate.

BRI module
The BRI module itself requires no particular settings and can be inserted into slot one straight out of the box. Once installed, it should work with all the default settings.

Diagram showing back view of the U50

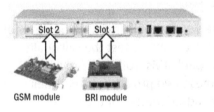

GSM MODULE SETTINGS

Once both modules are properly installed, plug the U50 back and power up. Once the U50 is up and running again, log in and click "Operator" to open the operators view page, the two SIMs should be working and displaying their signal strengths. Both suppliers signals appear to be good.

Status	Signal Strength	Type	Port	BLF Label
Connected	ıll	GSM	1	Channel1
Connected	ıll	GSM	2	Channel2

Next go to "Basic", "Trunks" and click "FXO/GSM.

Enter the settings as below:-

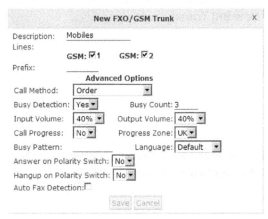

Click "Save" to finish. The screen will display the GSM trunk you have just created, the trunk will allow calls to mobiles via the SIMs.

List of Trunks		New FXO/GSM Trunk	
	Trunk Name	FXO/GSM Ports	Options
1	Mobiles	2	Edit Delete

BRI MODULE SETTINGS

In order for the settings and connections to be tested, it is was decided to do this after hours as it involves connecting the current ISDN lines to the U50. To do this, unplug the two network cables (connected to the BT ISDN boxes) from the back of the current PBX and plug into port 1 and 2 of the BRI module in the U50.

The operators view page should display the following:-

BRI module		
Status	Type	Port
Connected	TE	1
Connected	TE	2

Now go to "Basic", "Trunk" and choose "BRI Trunks" and click "New BRI Trunk", to add a "New BRI Trunk".

Enter settings as below, make sure the "Lines" match the ports that the ISDN network cables are plugged into.

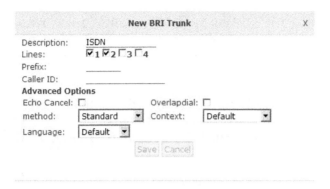

Leave all settings as default at this stage and click "Save". The screen should now display the following:-

Confirm that all inbound calls will be answered by the "Queue" i.e. extension 630. The U50 should be configured to receive all incoming calls by now.

Several dozens of trial calls are made to the 2 mobile numbers (GSM module) as well as the main office number (BRI module). This is to test the call qualities of mobile calls as well as standard landline calls to the ISDN lines.

Several staff has been asked to use their mobile phones to call the two mobile numbers more than a dozen times, the result indicates that the call quality is as good as any mobile phones with no delays or echoes experienced.

Remote office made several landline calls to the main office number and several dozen calls to the main landline number was made from staff mobile phones and standard telephones of remote staff at home.

Surprisingly, slightly echoing was experienced with most of the calls. Although the volume of the echoing was not high, the issue must be addressed before the system is launched properly. To try to remove the echo issue, "Echo Cancel" will be enabled on the BRI Trunk. Go to "Basic", "Trunk" and choose "BRI Trunks". "Edit" the "ISDN" trunk settings as below:-

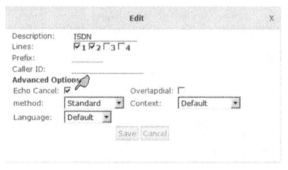

Click "Save" to finish. A dozen more calls were made to the main office landline again, this time, all calls sounded good with no one experiencing echoing problems.

The system is now ready to make outgoing calls, but first of all, we need to create the correct "Dial Rules" and "Dial Patterns". The U50 can only make calls if there is a "Dial Rule" and the numbers dialled must match the ("Dial Pattern") within the "Dial Rule". For the initial trial, the "Dial Rule" Standard allows for just about any number to be dialled successfully using the available "SIP Trunk", so this dial rule must be either removed or modified. Since the U50 has three usable trunks by now, it will require one or more "Dial Rules" to logically place these calls. In addition, when the remote office comes on line, there will be a requirement to include internal extensions to enable dialling between extension of both offices.

In order to make calls by using the cheapest and most appropriate method of calling, each "Dial Rule" must be configured with "Dial Patterns" to utilise the correct trunks to make outgoing calls. For example, to call a mobile number, the cheapest outgoing route is to use one of the mobile SIMs with a prepaid unlimited minutes package. The first "Dial Rule" ("Standard") should include "Dial Patterns" that is configured as follows:-

- dialling a number starting with 07 followed by nine numbers will result in the call routed via an available SIM channel in the GSM trunk (mobile calls)
- dialling a number starting with 01, 02, 03, 05, 07, 08 followed by nine numbers will result in the call routed via an ISDN line in the ISDN trunk (national calls)
- dialling a number starting from 2 to 6 followed by six numbers will result in the call routed via an ISDN line in the ISDN trunk (local calls)
- no "Dial Patterns" for international (00) or (09) premium rate numbers

By modifying the current "Dial Rule" Standard, the routing of calls to the correct trunk can be achieved. Go to the left hand menu, choose "Basic", "Outbound Rules" and click on "Dial Rules". Then click on the "+" sign as below to add another rule.

This rule is for calls to mobiles, enter settings to something similar below:-

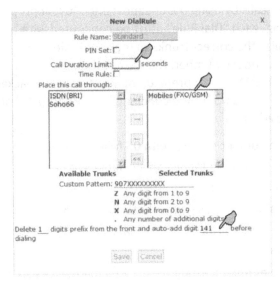

The above rule works like the following:

- "Call Duration Limit" is not specified, can be as long as necessary
- the call is placed through the trunk "Mobiles (FXO/GSM)"
- do this for any calls that starts with 907 and followed by nine numbers (0 - 9)
- remove the first digit i.e. 9 and add 141 to the beginning (number withheld)

Note that when a call is placed, the actual number dialled by the user is compared with the "Dial Patterns" in each route (from highest to lowest priority) until a match is found. In the case above, an extension dialling a number starting with 907, the system will try to use an available SIM channel first, if no SIMs channels are available, trunk using ISDN will be used.

For calls to national numbers, the "ISDN (BRI)" trunk will be used. The settings should be something like below:-

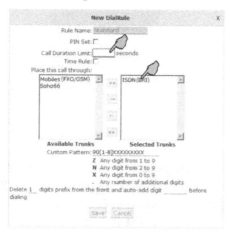

The above "Custom Pattern" means any number dialled beginning with 90 followed by a number between 1 and 8 and then followed by nine numbers will be routed over the "ISDN (BRI)" trunk. Note that this will include, mobile numbers starting with 07 too, but the "Custom Pattern" for the "Mobile (FXO/GSM)" trunk is higher in priority. The "ISDN (BRI)" trunk will only be used to dial 07 numbers if the "Mobile (FXO/GSM)" trunk is not available.

For dialling local numbers, the "Custom Patterns" will be something like 9[2-6]XXXXXX which means dialling the area code of (0191) for local calls is not required.

It is a good idea to include the emergency number 999 as part of the dial plan, "Custom Pattern" of something like 99XX should allow the emergency number to be placed through the ISDN (BRI) trunk.

The trunk for VOIP provider Soho66 is not included in any of the rules because the intension is to use this provider for incoming calls only, but it can be changed should the need arise.

When complete, the screen should look something like the one below:-

The U50 configuration is complete and is ready to be rolled out fully. The next stage is to implement all the SIP Phones, remote SIP Phones and mobile phone app as shown previously. Once all of these devices are configured, the U50 takes over as the PBX for the company.

SETTING UP THE U50 FOR THE REMOTE OFFICE
The process of rolling out the remote office VOIP system is identical to the main office, of course, there is no longer any need to test call qualities, call flows etc. The remote office VOIP system will be:-

- U50 configured to be on the remote office LAN with settings appropriate for the remote office (set "Primary" and "Alternate" DNS servers to cover internet failures)
- extensions range starts at 601
- 2 ISDN channels and 2 GSM channels
- voicemail will be sent by a smart host (mail.acme.co.uk)

All settings for the U50 and the Grandstream SIP Phones are as shown in the previous sections, the only exception is the sending of voicemail by emails. Since the remote office does not have local email server, it is therefore necessary to use an external email server to send voicemails.

ACME Ltd. uses a mail server mail.acme.co.uk which is configured as a smart host for the main office Exchange server to send external emails, so the "SMTP Server" settings of the U50 should be like below:-

After completing all settings for the U50 and installed all the SIP Phones as specified in earlier sections, the remote office VOIP system is operational. All that is left now is to created a trunk (link between the offices) and integrate the two systems.

MAIN OFFICE PEER MODE SIP TRUNK

The U50 of the main office requires a VOIP trunk to be created, use standard process to create a "New VOIP Trunk". Tick the "Peer Mode" tick box (note that when "peer Mode" is ticked, the "Host" field disappears, enter settings to something like below:-

Leave "Maximum Channels" at "0" which means no limit. Set "Username" and "Authuser" to "mainoffice", the "Password" will be the same as the U50 (strong password).

REMOTE OFFICE SIP TRUNK TO MAIN OFFICE

The U50 at the remote office requires a "VOIP" Trunk that is configured to register with the "VOIP Trunk" previously created at the main office. Add a "New VOIP Trunk" by using the normal process, the settings should be like below:-

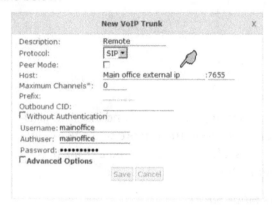

The "Host" field should be the external ip address of the main router at the main office. The "Password" should be the one set at the "VOIP Trunk" set previously in the U50 at the main office. Click "Save" to finish.

At the main office, the operator's view page should display something like the following:-

At the remote office, the operator's view page should display something the following:-

VoIP Trunks

Status	Trunk Name	Type	Username	Hostname/IP/Port	Reachability
Registered	Remote	SIP	mainoffice	Main Office IP :7655	OK (80 ms)

The two systems are now integrated, the next stage is to create dial rules so that the two systems can dial each other.

For the main office, create a dial rule using the "Main" trunk created previously. The settings should be something similar to below:-

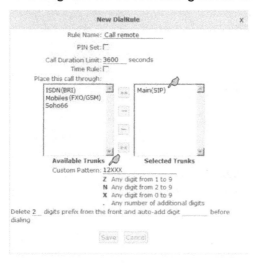

The "Custom Pattern" is 12XXX, this means that in order to call the remote office, dial 12 followed by three numbers. For example, to dial extension 601 at the remote office, dial 12601. The system will remove the first two digits i.e. 12 and dials 601. This rule is fine for dialling extensions at the remote office, but it will not allow for dialling external numbers through the remote office VOIP system. By putting a "." after the last "X" in the "Custom Pattern" i.e. "12XXX.", main office extensions will be allowed to make external calls through the remote office system. However, to call external numbers this way will require a "9" after the "12".

Make sure the an appropriate "Dial Plan" is chosen i.e. one that can make external calls. Now, the "Call remote" rule must be included in the relevant "Dial Plan" i.e. "DialPlan1". To do so, go to "DialPlan1" and tick the "Call remote" tick box and click "Save".

Now the remote office will also need a "Dial Rule" in order to dial extensions at the main office. The process is exactly the same as with the main office U50, except the "Dial Rule" is configured to use the "Remote (SIP)" trunk to connect to the main office.

The same convention can be used for dialling the main office extensions e.g. calling extension 201 will mean dialling 12201 from the remote office.

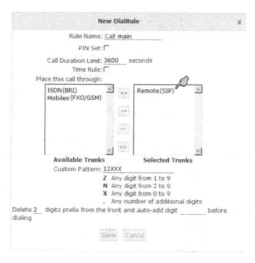

Finally, add the "Dial Rule" to "DialPlan1" of the remote office U50 like below:-

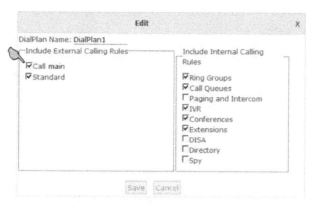

Click "Save" to finish. The two office phone systems are now fully integrated and can dial or transfer calls between each other. Although it is possible to make external calls through the other VOIP system, it has been decided that there is no requirement for such function, so the "Custom Pattern" remains and external calls through the other PBX will not be possible.

The remote office U50 will be configured for all incoming calls to go to their reception i.e. extension 601. If the call is not answered within 30 seconds, or if the extension is engaged, calls will be forwarded to 602 and 603. Alternatively, if extension 601 is unmanned, any other extension can pick up the call by pressing **601.

After putting a permanent divert (done online) for the current main office landline number to the VOIP number supplied by Soho66, all incoming calls to the landline will be diverted to the VOIP number (5 lines) and calls will be answered by reception at main office. The two VOIP systems are able to work as one integrated system where calls to one office means it can be transferred to an extension in either of one the offices as well as remote workers.

DIAGRAM SHOWING THE NEW CALL FLOW:-

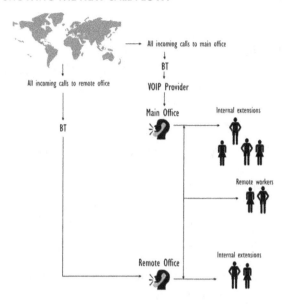

All incoming calls to remote office

BT

All incoming calls to main office

BT

VOIP Provider

Main Office

Internal extensions

Remote workers

Remote Office

Internal extensions

FINAL WORDS

The systems have been working reliably for the past six months now and the company has been benefitting from a feature rich system and the massive cost savings!

CHAPTER 9

BRIEF BACKGROUND INFORMATION FOR THE BEGINNERS

Most of us are familiar with the terms and "The Internet" and "LAN", especially if you have more than one device to access the internet at home. You effectively will have a LAN in your home and devices in your LAN are connected to The Internet .

ABOUT THE INTERNET

"The Internet" is a global system of interconnected computer networks that also use the standard *TCP/IP* (Transmission Control Protocol/Internet Protocol) to link several billion devices worldwide. It is often confused with the "World Wide Web", where we search for information by using search engines like "Google", purchase products on e-Commerce sites and socialise with friends on the likes of "Facebook" etc. Nowadays, when people talk about the internet, they usually mean the world wide web. Looking back at the origins of the internet, its main purpose was anything but social!! The main aim of DARPA—Defence Advanced Research Projects Agency that invented the original concept of internet was to decentralise their network (ARPANet). This meant that in the event of a nuclear war, even if the computer system in one site was destroyed, there would still be communication between all the other computers.

ABOUT LANs

A local area network (LAN) is a group of devices connected together by cables or wireless to form a private network within one location. Typically, devices on a LAN will connect to a router or a switch, which is responsible for passing data between these devices. For businesses, the LAN would allow different users to share available resources like printers, faxes etc. The standard protocol used on a LAN is also TCP/IP.

ABOUT TCP/IP

TCP/IP is a protocol for sending data packets which ensures that these packets of data are sent and ultimately received where they need to go, and in turn assembled in the proper order so that the data sent is exactly the same as the data received.

Transmission Control Protocol (TCP) provides reliable, ordered, and error-checked delivery of a stream of ip addresses in the form of octets between applications running on hosts communicating over an IP network.

Internet Protocol (IP) is the principal communications protocol for relaying datagram across network boundaries. Its routing function enables internetworking essential to how The Internet works.

About VOIP

Voice over IP (**VoIP**) is a technology for sending voice over a digital network. The network can be a LAN or The Internet. VOIP is very often confused with Internet Telephony which also makes use of The Internet .

How does VOIP work?

Elements of basic operation of VoIP, where the input signal derives from a conventional analogue telephone. The output of this is through a codec (compression decompression), data consists of IP packets that are transmitted on the Web or other data circuit for delivery to the distant end. A codec is a device or program that compresses data to enable faster transmission and decompresses received data. Typical format for audio codec are G.711, G.722.2, G.729 etc.

Diagram showing a simplistic picture of how VOIP works

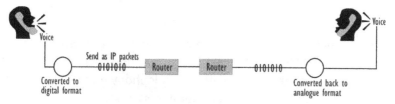

At the far end, the IP packets are input to a converter that strips off the IP header, stores the payload, and then releases it in a constant bit stream to a codec. Of course, this codec must be compatible with its near-end counterpart. The codec converts the digital bit stream back to an analogue signal that is input to a standard telephone.

DIAGRAM SHOWING HOW **VOIP** WORKS BY USING **GSM, PSTN** AND **IP** TELEPHONY

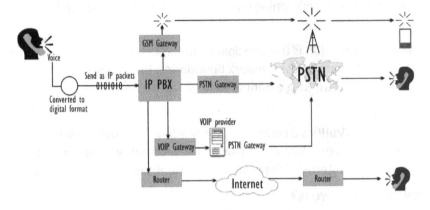

A user connected to an IP PBX can make calls to:-

- mobile networks by using the GSM Gateway
- PSTN (normal telephone lines) by using a local PSTN Gateway
- a VOIP provider
- another VOIP user or VOIP PBX over The Internet

ABOUT SIP

The Session Initiation Protocol(SIP) is a communications protocol for signalling and controlling multimedia communication sessions. The most common applications of SIP are in Internet telephony for voice and video calls, as well as instant messaging all over IP networks.

In IP and traditional telephony, there are two phases to a telephone call. The first phase is "call setup," and includes all of the details needed to get two telephones talking. Once the call has been setup, the phones enter a "data transfer" phase of the call using RTP (the Real-time Transport Protocol) to actually send the voice data between phones.

SIP also has great breadth as it does more than just handle call setup. The table below shows the five major functions within SIP from a VoIP point of view.

Function	Description
User location and registration	End points (telephones) notify SIP proxies of their location; SIP determines which end points will participate in a call.
User availability	SIP is used by end points to determine whether they will "answer" a call.
User capabilities	SIP is used by end points to negotiate media capabilities, such as agreeing on a mutually supported voice codec.
Session setup	SIP tells the end point that its phone should be "ringing;" SIP is used to agree on session attributes used by the calling and called party.
Session management	SIP is used to transfer calls, terminate calls, and change call parameters in mid-session (such as adding a 3-way conference).

SIP Phones are often called VoIP Phones or Soft phones. These are telephones that use VoIP technologies for making calls over an IP Network or the traditional PSTN networks. There are two types of SIP Phones. Hardware phones are actually telephones just like normal telephones and Soft Phones are software applications that run on computers or mobile devices like smart phones or tablets. SIP Phones use the SIP protocol and to make calls over IPv4 and IPv6 networks and can use either TCP or UDP.

About UDP

User Datagram Protocol is a communications protocol that offers a limited amount of service when messages are exchanged between computers in a network that uses the Internet Protocol (IP).

What has UDP got to do with VOIP when we have been talking about TCP?

Surprisingly, real time communications services such as VoIP do not require a completely reliable transport layer protocol like TCP. Because of the requirement of TCP to establish a connection between two end points and sending data in the correct order and without error, unacceptable delays can occur causing delays and jittering. Since packet loss usually only have minor impacts on the audio output, it is much better to drop a packet and have a few milliseconds of silence than to have seconds of lag.

UDP and Ports

Every computer or device on the Internet must have a unique number assigned to it called the IP address. This IP address is used to locate your particular device e.g. IP PBX out of the millions of other devices connected to the Internet. When another device like a SIP Phone tries to communicate with your IP PBX, your IP PBX accepts the communication data by using TCP or UDP ports. The UDP protocol provides port numbers to help distinguish different user requests.

UDP Ports and firewalls

As with almost every devices that requires internet access within a LAN, an IP PBX will be located behind a firewall. The UDP protocol does not traverse firewalls very well at all. This raises the issue that in order to carry out a two way conversation, the call must be set up and voice data transmitted through the firewall (usually NAT - network address translation).

STUN SERVER

A STUN server(Session Traversal of User Datagram Protocol)through Network Address Translators (NAT) allows NAT clients (i.e. SIP Phones behind a firewall) to setup phone calls to a VoIP provider hosted outside of the local network.

FIREWALL PORT FORWARDING

Typically, SIP servers like Asterisk use port 5060 for UDP and ports used for RTP communications are dynamically negotiated by SIP when a new VoIP session is established. The range can be between 10000 to 20000. It is often necessary to open ports on the firewall and forward packets to the IP PBX in order for the VOIP system to work correctly e.g. one way audio is often solved this way . For RTP communications, up to four ports may be required for one call, so to allow for ten simultaneous calls, forty ports will be required to be open on the firewall. The IP PBX needs to specify which port range is required e.g. 10000 - 10040 matched by port forwarding in at the firewall.

If the IP PBX is set up to accept registrations from outside the LAN e.g. a remote office trunk, then port forwarding from a different port e.g. port 7655 from the firewall to port 5060 of the IP PBX. The reason for changing the default port is to discourage hackers from easily hacking into the IP PBX.

ABOUT SKYPE™ PROTOCOL

SKYPE™ protocol is a peer-to-peer Internet telephony protocol used to move encrypted voice over IP (VoIP) traffic between SKYPE™ members' computers (peers).

SKYPE™ uses RC4 encryption for signalling and AES for voice data. The protocol is proprietary, created specifically for SKYPE™ sessions, and does not work with most standard VoIP networks without licensing from SKYPE™

COMMON TERMS USED IN VOIP

ATA - Analogue Telephone Adaptor - This is a small adaptor, usually about the size of a cigarette packet, that you plug into a normal phone to allow it to connect to a VoIP network and send calls over the Internet.

Bandwidth - Is the amount or volume of data that can be transmitted over an Internet or communication line in a given amount of time. It is measured in bits per second (bps) e.g., 10 mbps for Internet speed, and Hertz (Hz) for phone/analogue systems. The higher the number, the faster communication will be.

BRI - Basic Rate Interface - BRI is an ISDN configuration mainly used for voice-grade telephone service. BRI provides 2 bearer channels (B channels) which are capable of carrying data, voice and other services.

CAT 5 - Category 5 cable is a twisted pair cable for carrying data signal typically used for computer and telephone networks.

Codec - In the world of VoIP a codec is used to encode voice for transmission access IP networks. Codec's for VoIP use are also referred to as vocoders, for "voice encoders". Codecs generally provide a compression capability to save network bandwidth. Some codecs also support silence suppression, where silence is not encoded or transmitted.

CTI – Computer Telephone Integration - This system allows your phones to interact with computers. An example is the ability to make a call directly from Outlook, or send voice mail to your inbox.

DHCP - Dynamic Host Configuration Protocol - DHCP is a protocol used by networked computers (clients) to obtain IP addresses and other parameters such as the default gateway, subnet mash, and IP addresses of DNS servers from a DHCP server. The DHCP server ensures that all IP addresses are unique.

DNS - Domain Name System - Domain Name Servers are like telephone directories. They maintain a directory of domain names e.g. it-etc.co.uk and translate them to Internet Protocol (IP) addresses.

DDI – Direct Dial In - Is a function of VoIP and some POTS, whereby a caller can directly call a phone on a desk instead of having to go through the PBX and answering system.

DID - Direct Inward Dialling - Direct Inward Dialling is a feature offered by telephone companies for use with their customers PBX systems, whereby the telephone company (TELCO) allocates a range of numbers all connected to their customer's PBX. As calls are presented to the PBX, the number that the caller dialled is also given, so the PBX can route the call to the desired person within the organization.

DTMF - Dual-tone Multi-Frequency - DTMF signalling is used for telephone signalling over the line in the voice frequency band to the call switching centre. The version of DTMF used for telephone tone dialling is known as the trademarked term Touch-Tone.

G.711 - G.711 is an ITU-T standard for audio compression. It is primarily used in telephony. G.711 represents logarithmic pulse-code modulation (PCM) samples for signals of voice frequencies, sampled at the rate of 8000 samples/second.

G729 - G.729 is an audio data compression algorithm for voice that compresses voice audio in chunks of 10 milliseconds. Music or tones such as DTMF or fax tones cannot be transported reliably with this codec, and thus use G.711 or out-of-band methods to transport these signals.

GSM- Global System for Mobile communication is a digital mobile telephony system that is widely used in Europe.

IP Address - An IP address is a unique address that certain electronic devices use in order to identify and communicate with each other on a computer network utilising the Internet Procotol standard. Any participating network device can have their own unique address.

IP PBX - Internet Protocol Private Branch Exchange - telephone switching system within an organisation) that switches calls between VoIP (voice over Internet Protocol or IP)

ISDN - Integrated Services Digital Network- is a set of CCITT/ITU standards for digital transmission over ordinary telephone copper wire as well as over other media.

IVR - Interactive Voice Response - IVR or interactive voice response is a phone technology that allows a computer to detect voice and touch tones using a normal phone call. The IVR system can respond with pre-recorded or dynamically generated audio to further direct callers on how to proceed. IVR systems can be used to control almost any function where the interface can be broken down into a series of simple menu choices.

PBX - Private Branch Exchange - PBX stands for Private Branch eXchange which operates as a connection between a private organisation and the public switched telephone network (PSTN). It is a system which connects the outside telephone network to the internal telephones, fax machines and extensions within the business. Often a PBX will include features like speed dial, conference calling and music on hold.

PoE - Power over Ethernet - Power over Ethernet is a technology used to transmit electrical power along with data to remote devices over standard Ethernet cable in a network. This technology is useful for powering IP telephones or network cameras where it would be costly to run power separately.

POTS - Plain Old Telephone System - POTS is a term which means voice grade telephone service that remains the basic form of residential and business telephone service in most parts of the world. Since the introduction of POTS more advanced forms of telephone service such as ISDN, mobile phones and voice over ip have been introduced. It has been available almost since the introduction of the public telephone system.

PSTN - Public Switched Telephone Network - The public switched telephone network is the network of the world's public circuit switched telephone networks. Originally the PSTN was a network of analogue telephone systems but now the PSTN is entirely digital. The PSTN is largely governed by technical standards created by the ITU-T and uses E.163/E.164 address (commonly known as telephone numbers) for addressing.

RTP - Real-time Transport Protocol - RTP defines a standardized packet format for delivering audio and video over the Internet.

Router - A router is a device that determines the proper path for data to travel between different networks and forwards data packets to the next device along this path. They connect networks together; a LAN to a WAN for example, to access the Internet. Routers are available in both wireless and wired versions.

SIP Phones - These are telephones that use the SIP protocol, commonly used in a VOIP system. They can be either hardware telephone or a software application that connects either locally or over the internet to an IP PBX.

SRTP – Secure Real-time Transfer Protocol - This creates a unique encryption code for each call, which makes eavesdropping nearly impossible, without reducing call quality.

Switch - A network switch is a computer networking device that connects network segments. Network switches are capable of inspecting data packets as they are received, determining the source and destination of that packet, and forwarding it appropriately. By delivering each message only to the connected device it was intended for, a network switch conserves network bandwidth and offers generally better performance than a hub.

uLaw and aLaw - The G.711 standard used by US and Europe respectively.

UPS - Uninterruptable Power Supply - is an electrical apparatus that provides emergency power to a load when the input power source, typically mains power, fails.

WAV Format - Waveform Audio File Format (WAVE, or more commonly known as WAV due to its filename extension) is a Microsoft and IBM audio file format standard for storing an audio bitstream on PCs.

www.ingramcontent.com/pod-product-compliance
Lightning Source LLC
Chambersburg PA
CBHW071156050326
40689CB00011B/2129